"Manuscipe"
The Anderson Family Legacy

By

Brian Keith Anderson

"MANUSCIPE"

" THE ANDERSON FAMILY LEGACY "

by:

Brian Keith Anderson

****

The Anderson Family Legacy

© 2025 Brian Keith Anderson

All rights reserved. No part of this book may be reproduced, stored in a retrieval system, or transmitted in any form or by any means—electronic, mechanical, photocopying, recording, or otherwise—without prior written permission of the author, except for brief quotations used in reviews or critical articles.

ISBN: 979-8-9996886-4-4

Printed in the United States of America

First Edition, 2025

Dedication

To the Andersons—past, present, and future.

May these pages honor your struggles, celebrate your triumphs,

and preserve your stories for generations yet to come.

Preface

*This book is not cold chronology. It is a living manuscript—a **Manuscipe**—woven with emotion, resilience, and identity.*

I chose the word Manuscipe because creating this work has been like preparing a recipe, handed down through generations. Each ingredient matters, the spices, the photographs, are the yeast that makes the past rise and breathe again. When blend together with patience, memories, and love, they become more than history on a page—they become nourishment for the soul of a family.

The story of the Anderson family is not just a record of names and dates, but a living history that connects us across time and place. When I began this journey, I set out to preserve the memories of our ancestors, so that future generations would know where they came from and the lives that shaped who we are today.

This book reflects years of research, conversations, and countless hours spent gathering documents, stories, and photographs. It is both a tribute to those who came before us and a gift to those who will carry the Anderson legacy forward.

I owe deep gratitude to family members who shared their memories, to archives and libraries that preserved our history, and to the guiding spirit that inspired me to bring this work into being. Without such support, this book would not have been possible.

It is my hope that *The Anderson Family Legacy* will serve as a bridge between the past and the present, reminding us that our family's story is also part of the greater story of America. May it inspire reflection, connection, and pride in the roots that bind us together.

— *Brian Keith Anderson*

2025

"We all carry within us the people who came before us."

— Liam Callanan

Table of Contents

Introduction: Why I Wrote This Manuscipe 2

Dedication 3

Acknowledgments 4

Family Motto & Author's Note 5

Part I: Exposition 7

The Land Before Us: Tennessee Roots 8

The First Andersons in America 10

From Sweden to Fort Christina 12

The Story of Anders Jöransson 14

Ericus Jöransson Andersson: The Bridge Between Worlds 16

Part II: Rising Action 18

Peter Anderson and the Move South 19

North Carolina to Tennessee: A Family in Motion 21

John Watson Anderson: The Horseman of the Ridge 23

Nathaniel Hamilton Anderson: The Civil Son 25

Edgar Anderson: The Gentleman Farmer 27

Part III: Climax 29

Abb Anderson: The Grit in the Grain 30

Robert Kenneth Anderson: The Quiet Foundation 32

Helen Maxine Adams: The Heart of the Home 34

The Anderson Children: Kenny, Kelly, Karen, Keith, and Kim 36

Part IV: Falling Action 38

The Grain Belt Years: Kokomo & Woodall 39

Returning to Henry's Cove 41

The Legacy of Labor and Land 43

The Inheritance of Memory 45

Part V: Resolution 47

Meeting Janice Walcek: A Living Thread 48

Canadian Connection 50

Final Reflections: What We Leave Behind 52

The Torchbearer's Oath 54

I am a storyteller, a researcher, and most importantly—a descendant of lives worth remembering. What began as a curiosity about my lineage grew into a mission: to give voice to those who came before me so that their triumphs, struggles, and humanity would not be forgotten.

You will find documented dates and places, yes, but also the whispers of family lore, the grit in ordinary lives, and the grace in enduring love.

I invite you not just to read, but to feel. To stand in the shoes of our ancestors. To reflect on the paths, they paved and the legacy they left—one that flows through each of us today.

History, for me, has never been just dates and names inked in dusty registers. It has always lived in the cadence of a grandfather's tale, in the handwritten letters folded into keepsake boxes, and in the pauses where memory falters but feeling remains. Manuscipe is the result of years spent listening, learning, and lovingly preserving those threads of our family's story.

My name is Brian Keith Anderson. I am a storyteller, a researcher, and most importantly—a descendant of lives worth remembering. What began as a curiosity about my lineage grew into a mission: to give voice to those who came before me so that their triumphs, struggles, and humanity would not be forgotten.

Anderson Family Line (Direct)

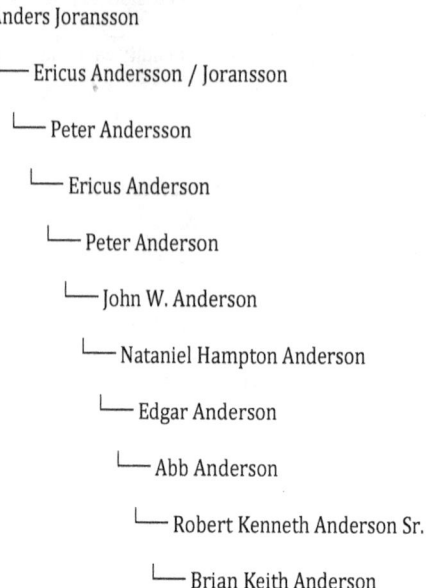

Anders Joransson
└── Ericus Andersson / Joransson
    └── Peter Andersson
        └── Ericus Anderson
            └── Peter Anderson
                └── John W. Anderson
                    └── Nataniel Hampton Anderson
                        └── Edgar Anderson
                            └── Abb Anderson
                                └── Robert Kenneth Anderson Sr.
                                    └── Brian Keith Anderson

From Anderson Family Legacy by Brian Keith Anderson

The sun hung low over the hills of southern Tennessee, casting long shadows across red clay fields worked by calloused hands for generations. A whippoorwill called out in the hush between day and dusk, its cry carrying through swaying pines and over the weathered rooftops of homes built by grit and kinship.

This was not just a place of birth and burial—it was a cradle of memory. Here, in soil turned by mule-drawn plows and beneath rafters warmed by hearth fires, the Anderson family carved its legacy. Seasons came and went, baptizing each generation in hardship, joy, and quiet perseverance.

Inside these pages lie the voices of those who rose with dawn and folded hope into every day's work. Some were soldiers, some were farmers, some were dreamers with ink-stained fingers or quilt-stitched prayers. Each story echoes with pride, resilience, and the enduring rhythm of family—threaded across time like a patchwork of shared blood and borrowed strength.

Step into this legacy not as a reader, but as a witness. Listen close, and you just might hear the creak of a porch swing, the laughter around a supper table, or the hush of reverent silence in a home built on memory. This is where the Anderson story unfolds.

Mid-1800s: A Land Newly Settled

The year was 1856, and the hills of Tennessee stretched wide and wild, dotted by saplings and dreams still taking root. The Anderson homestead stood near a bend in the creek, its foundation laid by hands calloused from building both shelter and hope. Chickens clucked in the yard, and the scent of fresh-cut timber mingled with cornbread rising in a cast-iron skillet. A wind carried voices across the hollow—some in prayer, some in laughter—but all anchored in beginnings. This was the dawn of the Anderson legacy.

🦋 Civil War Era: A House Divided

By 1863, the landscape had changed. Cannon smoke had ghosted the sky, and songs of peace gave way to marching drums. Within the Anderson household, brothers whispered on opposite sides of history, one donning Union blue, another Southern gray. The front porch, once a place for storytelling, now bore silent worry. Fields lay fallow, yet hearts grew fiercely rooted in conviction, faith, and kin. History's fire did not burn the family down—it tempered their steel.

🪶 1900s: A Return to the Land

After hardship, prosperity crept in not with thunder, but with the steady rhythm of plows and hymnals. The year was 1908. Children chased fireflies through fields that had once borne blood but now yielded corn, laughter, and renewal. Great-grandmother's quilt hung on the line, each patch a memory sewn from hardship and celebration. At supper, stories flowed as freely as sweet tea, tying the young to names they would never meet but always honor.

🧶 Great Depression: Grit and Grace

The 1930s arrived lean and dust laden. The Andersons, like so many, stretched a dollar as far as it would go—but never their dignity. Soup pots simmered low, yet no visitor left hungry. Papa read Bible verses aloud while Mama stitched life into fraying seams. Hope came not from gold, but from grit: a promise passed down like a family heirloom that said, "We are Andersons. We endure. We rise."

🔒 Modern Reflection: The Inheritance of Memory

Now, generations later, the pages of this book serve as both mirror and lantern. The landscape may be more paved, the tools more digital—but the soil of legacy remains rich beneath our feet. Through each story, each name, and every dusty photo, the pulse of the past beats steadily in the present. This is not simply our history. It is our inheritance.

John Watson Anderson Founding Father of Coffee County Tennessee

📝 Brian Keith Anderson — The Son Who Listened

Brian Keith Anderson was born in McMinnville, Tennessee, and raised on the red clay of Hillsboro, where memory clings to the land like dew on morning grass. He did not just inherit a name—he inherited a calling.

A quiet observer with reverence for the past, Brian became the family's historian not by title, but by instinct. Through years of listening, researching, and writing, he transformed fading stories into a living legacy. His Manuscipe is more than a book, it is a bridge between generations.

In these pages, Brian is not just the author. He is the voice of those who came before, and the torchbearer for those yet to come.

🩶 Robert Kenneth Anderson----The Quiet Foundation

Born in 1932 in Hillsboro, Tennessee, Robert Kenneth Anderson came of age in a world shifting fast—but he moved through it with steady hands and a grounded heart. He was a man who believed in doing things right the first time, in showing love through action, and in letting his work speak louder than words.

🧂 Abb Anderson (1906–1951) – The Grit in the Grain

The 1930s carved dust into the bones of the land, but Abb Anderson remained. A man of few words and many deeds, he carried worry like a weight in his shoulders and love like warmth in his cornbread. His laugh rumbled like tractor engines, and his presence brought calm to chaotic times. Even in lean years, his faith never frayed—just mended itself silently in the seams of his overalls and the rhythm of routine.

🏛 Edgar Anderson (1874–1955) – The Gentleman Farmer

With one hand on the Bible and the other on the reins of a plow horse, Edgar straddled two eras—old customs and new inventions. He wrote poetry in the margins of seed catalogues and taught his children to dance between tradition and progress. A pressed collar and polished boots did not hide the dirt beneath his nails; dignity, for Edgar, lived in action. And every action spoke of home, honor, and harvest.

🎖 Nathaniel Hamilton Anderson (1837–1919) – The Civil Son

Born into shadow and raised into battle, Nathaniel watched Tennessee split under the weight of war. A teenager, when shots were first fired, and He carried both youthful idealism and adult exhaustion long before gray streaked his hair. After the war, he did not seek applause—he rebuilt fence lines and families and planted peace where division had once taken root. The silence in his old age spoke louder than any sermon.

John Watson Anderson (1806–1879) – The Horseman of the Ridge

They say John Watson could read a trail like a scripture and tell the weather by the twitch of his mule's ear. He was born with wild Tennessee hills in his veins and lived by rhythm: sunrise, livestock, rain, and prayer. His journal, now worn and yellowing, holds tales of births, storms, and bargains struck with a handshake. His was a world of frontiers—both literal and spiritual—and he stood at every crossing with steadfast grace.

Peter Anderson (1765–1824) – The Patriot's Son

Peter was a boy during the Revolution and a man before Tennessee had borders. He spoke with a Swedish lilt his father never let fade and taught his sons to clear land and quote Proverbs. His homestead was made of logs and loyalty—anchored on love, faith, and hard-earned land. With every split-rail fence, Peter declared his family's right to belong and to build something that would outlast him.

Ericus Anderson (1737–1811) – The Artisan Settler

Ericus arrived not as a conqueror, but as a craftsman. His hands, once trained in Swedish joinery, found new rhythm in colonial soil. He built homes, forged friendships, and stitched his European past into the patchwork of the American frontier. In letters now faded, he wrote of "the good country" and of dreams born beneath unfamiliar stars. His legacy was carved not into monuments, but mantels and hearts.

Peter Ericsson Andersson (1706–1787) – The Immigrant Dreamer Who Kept Moving

"By the time Peter Anderson left Delaware, his hands were already calloused by labor and his heart seasoned by hope. He was not chasing a dream—he was building one, one move at a time. With a worn Bible and a settler's resolve, he turned south toward North Carolina, where the land was wild and the future unwritten."

Peter had long since made a living in Delaware, raising a family and working the soil. But as the colonies grew and land became scarce, he joined the wave of pioneers seeking new beginnings in the southern backcountry. North Carolina offered promise—untamed forests, fertile ground, and the chance to shape something lasting.

There, amid the rolling hills and whispering pines, Peter laid down new roots. He built a homestead, raised his children in faith and fortitude, and became a quiet patriarch of a growing legacy.

"His sons, raised on the edge of wilderness, inherited not just his name but his restlessness. They followed the ridgelines westward, crossing the Appalachian spine into the Tennessee frontier. Near what would become Statesville, they cleared land, raised cabins, and planted the Anderson name in soil that still remembers them."

Peter never saw Tennessee. But his spirit did. It traveled in the wagons of his sons, in the hymns they sang, and in the sweat, they poured into new land. He was the beginning of a journey that would stretch across centuries.

"He didn't need to see the hills of Tennessee to shape them. His legacy arrived before his name did—carried in the hearts of sons who believed, as he did, that the future was something you built with your own two hands."

💜 Ericus Jöransson Andersson (1671–1765) – The Swedish Emigrant's Son Who Took Root

"Born beneath the flag of New Sweden, Ericus Jöransson Andersson never crossed an ocean—but he carried the legacy of those who did. Born at Fort Christina in 1671, he was a child of the Delaware frontier, raised in the rhythms of river, forest, and faith. His life was not one of conquest, but of quiet endurance."

Ericus was born on May 13, 1671, in Fort Christina—modern-day Wilmington, Delaware—just as the Swedish colonial presence was fading into English control. His father, Anders Jöransson, had come from Sweden, but Ericus was among the first generation born in the Americas. He grew up along the Brandywine Creek, where Swedish customs mingled with English law and Lenape land.

He married Brita Bridget Paulsson in New Castle in 1687, and together they raised a large family—children who would carry the Andersson name into the next century, adapting it to Anderson as they moved with the frontier.

"Ericus never left Delaware, but his legacy did. His sons and grandsons would follow the call of open land, moving south into North Carolina and west into Tennessee. From the banks of the Brandywine, his bloodline flowed into the hills and hollers of Appalachia."

He died on March 25, 1765, at the age of ninety-three, having witnessed the transformation of his homeland from a Swedish outpost to a British colony on the brink of revolution. He was buried near the waters that had cradled his entire life.

"Ericus was not an immigrant, but a bridge—between old world and new, between Swedish roots and American branches. His story is not one of departure, but of deep belonging. In the soil of Delaware, he planted a legacy that would stretch far beyond its borders."

⚒ Anders Jöransson (1642–1690) – The Origin Point

"He crossed the Atlantic not as a free man, but as a servant with a dream. Anders Jöransson arrived in the Delaware Colony aboard the Swedish ship Kalmar Nyckel, a vessel of hope for many and hardship for most. Bound by indenture but driven by faith, he stepped ashore near Fort Christina and began the long work of turning servitude into stewardship."

Born in Sweden in 1645, Anders was part of the early wave of settlers who followed the New Sweden colony's promise of land and liberty. Though the colony would soon pass into Dutch and then English hands, Anders remained—rooted not in politics, but in purpose.

"After years of labor, Anders earned his freedom and claimed land on Deer Point, near present-day New Castle. There, he built a modest homestead, cleared fields with his own hands, and raised a family in the shadow of the Brandywine. What began in bondage became a legacy of liberty."

His son Ericus, born in 1671 at Fort Christina, would become the first generation of the family born on American soil. The Andersson name—later shortened to Anderson—would echo through the valleys of North Carolina and the hills of Tennessee.

****

"Anders never saw the frontier his descendants would cross, but he lit the first fire. He was the origin point—the man who turned hardship into heritage, and whose quiet triumph still echoes in the lives of those who bear his name."

"In the soil of Deer Point, Anders planted more than crops—he planted the Anderson legacy. And though his grave lies near the Delaware River, his story flows through every ridge and hollow his descendants would one day call home."

Brian Keith Anderson, Stone with W.H. Anderson craved it, He moved to Oklahoma, 1887

🔥 Brian Keith Anderson — The Torchbearer and Keeper of Memory

In a world where history often fades beneath screens and soundbites, Brian Keith Anderson chose preservation over forgetting. Born in McMinnville, Tennessee, near to the creeks and hollows his ancestors once tilled, Brian came into the world with history already coursing through his veins. Raised in the old homeplace of Abb and Willie Phillips Anderson, he grew up with the scent of clay soil, the rhythm of mule-drawn plows, and the quiet strength of kinship.

He was the kind of man who listened longer than he spoke—who could find meaning in a faded photograph, a forgotten recipe, or a whispered family tale. Whether seated in the stillness of early morning with dusty binders and coffee in hand, or walking the wooded hollows of Tennessee, Brian gathered moments like seeds—planting them in paragraphs so they might bloom again in the hands of his grandchildren's grandchildren.

Too many, he is a historian. To others, a storyteller. But within these pages, Brian becomes what every family needs most: a keeper of truth and a voice for the silenced. His ink is not just for the past—it is for the pulse that beats on through every Anderson bloodline that follows.

This Manuscipe is his act of devotion: not just to remember, but to revive. Not just to record, but to resurrect. He did more than inherited a name—he inherited a calling. And in answering it, he became both the torchbearer and the keeper of memory.

The picture on the left Started a journey for me to Oklahoma to find my Great Uncle, William Henry Anderson, who had left in 1887 to move to Norman, Oklahoma. He carved his initial's W.H. Anderson, Nov. 5th, 1887. I did not know who he was at the time. This set into motion to where I traveled there and finally found his grave.

Anderson, Meadows, Zumbro, Bennett, which was in Henry's Cove.

****

Brian Keith Anderson at old still, used by families; Anderson, Meadows, Zumbro, Bennetts (was looking around and found this jar in the spring that came down by it, I believe Uncle George wanted me to have this, I have it in my computer room at home.)

Name: Brian Keith Anderson Birthplace: Tennessee, United States Role: Author, historian, and guardian of the Anderson family legacy Interests: Genealogy, historical storytelling, cultural preservation Traits: Methodical, intuitive, emotionally rooted, dedicated to honoring those who came before Life's Work: Creator of Manuscript, a multigenerational narrative honoring the Anderson family from its Swedish roots to present-day Tennessee Legacy Mission: To preserve, document, and breathe life into the stories of his ancestors—not just for today, but for generations yet to come.

📜 *Profile: Brian Keith Anderson*

Full Name: Brian Keith Anderson

Date of Birth: January 7, 1958

Place of Birth: Tennessee, United States

Heritage: eleven -generation descendant of Swedish emigrant Anders Jöransson

Role: Author, historian, and preserver of family memory

Notable Work: *Manuscipe – The Anderson Family Legacy*

Passions: Genealogy, historical storytelling, and cultural preservation

"We endure. We rise."

🍃 The Hands That Carried Memory – The Story of Brian Keith Anderson

Born in McMinnville, Tennessee, near to the creeks and hollows his ancestors once tilled, Brian Keith Anderson came into the world with history already coursing through his veins. At the time, his family lived in Hillsboro in the old homeplace of Abb and Willie Phillips Anderson. It was a place that smelled of clay soil and mule sweat, of biscuits baked before sunrise and prayers whispered through storms. He would carry those smells, those echoes, for a lifetime.

At five, the road bent toward his grandmother Bessie Brown Adams's house—at the far end of Asbury Road. There, the rhythm of his youth was set, days in the fields, sunburnt skin, and dirt beneath fingernails that never quite washed away. His father, Robert Kenneth Anderson, farmed hard with R.L. Sherrill—raising cattle, hogs, potatoes, soybeans, white and yellow corn, and hay for the herds. It was not just work; it was an inheritance of purpose.

Summers were not for lazing. Young Brian worked as the potato grader and pulled corn with mules, loaded trucks of corn down to sell to Alabama's Farmers markets. His life was built from effort—honest and unrelenting.

When the Vietnam War cast its long shadow, Brian braced for the draft, but it halted just shy of his footsteps in 1973. With college off the table, he carved a different path—into trade school, into the circuits and wires of Electricity and Electronics. Within six months, he earned certification as a Commercial Electrician.

From there, life took him into the guts of Gold Kist Inc.—lifts, pulleys, motors, and wheat-dusted air. When Kokomo Grain took over, he stayed and stayed long, rising to Plant Supervisor while still wielding a wrench like gospel. Rye, malt, and corn moved through his firsthand the way to Jack Daniel's barrels. He was the quiet rhythm behind a Tennessee legend. After Kokomo lost Jack Daniel's contract and sold the elevator, the story did not end—it shifted. Brian found new footing with Woodall Grain Company, a name etched across seven elevators and countless sunrise starts. There, he became more than a technician, he became the trusted hands and seasoned mind behind the hum of operations spread across the region.

No longer managing a single site but maintaining a network, Brian's knowledge became the glue that held Woodall's infrastructure together. Maintenance. Electrical troubleshooting. Problem-solving when the storms hit or the machines groaned too loud to ignore. He traveled where he was needed, steadfast and capable.

In time, illness would ask for his tools to be set down—but not before he left his imprint on every grain belt he had ever touched. His retirement was not a retreat, it was a well-earned exhale, drawn in the same Tennessee hills where his ancestors first settled.

He returned to Henry's Cove, in 2004 the cradle of his kin since the 1840s. There, among the ridges and echoes, Brian did not simply rest—he reflected. Not on what had been lost to time, but what had been lovingly preserved through it.

****
**

Part 3: Climax

📖 Robert Kenneth Anderson (1932-2015)

"The Steadfast Son"

When the world was changing faster than fence posts could be set, Robert Kenneth Anderson stood firm. Born just months before the end of World War II, Robert came of age in a time of television antennas, shifting values, and mechanical wonder—but his heartbeat to the rhythm of older things: family, faith, and a job done right the first time.

His hands bore the marks of honest work, and his voice—gentle but resolute—carried authority learned from the soil and softened by kinship. The scent of oil and cedar followed him, a signature of time spent turning wrenches and splitting wood. He wore his responsibilities like his flannel shirts: unshowy, durable, and perfectly fitted.

Robert was the kind of father who showed love in action, a car always tuned; a roof always repaired before rain. But when he spoke, his words could still a room or lift a heart. Stories told from the porch swing were passed down like a scripture, humor edged with wisdom, memory stitched with meaning. He raised more than crops—he raised kin with quiet strength and an unshakable sense of place.

Though his name will not appear in textbooks, his legacy is inked in this one. Through every chapter in *Manuscript*, his steadiness whispers between the lines: Hold fast. Stand tall. Remember who you are.

Things that change the direction of the story. **Robert Kenneth Anderson Sr.** was born on February 25, 1932, in Hillsboro, Coffee County, Tennessee, and passed away on March 17, 2015, in the same town—having spent a lifetime walking, shaping, and honoring the land of his birth. Raised in a farming family, he inherited not only soil, but a quiet strength passed down through calloused hands and deep-rooted values. When his father died and his older brother was lost in World War II, he became head of the household far earlier than most. During the Korean War, he served overseas in Germany, where he worked on a U.S. Air Force base, managing records and base operations with diligence and integrity. Though eligible for VA benefits, he chose never to use them, saying, "I can pay for my insurance—let it go to someone who needs it more than I do." That was how he lived: quietly generous, never asking for more than he gave. After 25 years of farming, he retired—but rest did not suit him. A year later, I handed him a patron list from my job in the grain industry, and he picked up where he left off—this time selling seeds, fertilizers, sprays, and chemicals for a company in Manchester, Tennessee. But what he truly offered was not just product, it was trust. With decades of experience, he became a field companion to local farmers, walking their rows, studying their crops, and offering wisdom rooted in sweat and soil. The advice he gave was valued not because of titles, but because of truth. When my mother passed, that work became his purpose. And he never stopped. He worked until the day he died. I still meet farmers who say, "Your dad helped me so much—I miss him." One of the most enduring lessons he gave me still rings in my memory today: "Son, if you want anything in this life, you will have to work for it. I cannot give it to you." He did not say it with harshness—it was a gift, wrapped in gravel and grace. That is who he was: a man who served, provided, and shaped generations—not with speeches, but with steady footsteps and a life well lived.

1. Robert Kenneth Anderson Jr.

Born: August 4, 1953

Place of Birth: Hillsboro, Coffee County, Tennessee

Status: Living

Spouse: Sandra Kay Norton

Born: About 1954 **Place of Birth:** Coffee County, Tennessee, United States

Status: Living

2. Michael Kelly Anderson Sr.

Born: November 12, 1955

Place of Birth: Hillsboro, Coffee County, Tennessee

Status: Living

Spouse: Melinda Joy Keith   **Born:** 1954

Place of Birth: Coffee County, Tennessee, United States

Status: Living

Married: April 20, 1974, Coffee County, Tennessee

3. Karen Anderson Hampton

Born: November 14, 1956

Place of Birth: Hillsboro, Coffee County, Tennessee

Status: Living

Spouse: Phillip W. Hampton

Born: 1958

Place of Birth: Lexington, Fayette County, Kentucky, United States

Status: Living

4. Brian Keith Anderson

Born: January 7, 1958

Place of Birth: McMinnville, Warren County, Tennessee

Status: Living

5. Kimberly Lea Anderson

Born: January 16, 1963

Place of Birth: McMinnville, Warren County, Tennessee

Status: Living

Spouse: Mike Adams**Born:** 1966

Place of Birth: Manchester, Coffee County, Tennessee

Status: Living

"Mom chose to name each of us with a 'K'—Kenny, Kelly, Karen, Keith, and Kim—a quiet string tying us together, like beads on the same thread. In a household where identity was rooted in kinship, even our names spoke of unity.

Kenneth Wife: **Helen Maxine Adams**Born: 29 May 1934, Hillsboro, Coffee County, Tennessee Died: 28 September 2004, Nashville, Davidson County, Tennessee

"At the heart of our story is Helen Maxine Adams, born in the soft hills of Coffee County and later laid to rest in the rhythm of Wesley Chapel Cemetery, Viola, Tennessee. She was more than a mother—she was the thread that quietly tied us together. With names that echoed each other—Kenny, Kelly, Karen, Keith, Kim—she gave us both identity and unity. Her presence, like her choices, was intentional, enduring, and full of grace."

"

The Heart of the Home: In Tribute to My Mother

Helen Maxine AdamsBorn: May 29, 1934 – Hillsboro, Coffee County, Tennessee Died: September 28, 2004 – Nashville, Davidson County, Tennessee Tags: Motherhood & Faith Tennessee Roots Family Matriarch Grace & Endurance Adams Lineage

My mother, Helen Maxine Adams, was born on a spring morning in 1934 in the quiet community of Hillsboro, Tennessee. The town was small, but the values it instilled were deep—and she was raised on them like gospel. Kindness. Duty. Faith. Work. She carried those things in her bones, not just her memory.

She was the kind of woman who did not need to raise her voice to be heard. Her quiet presence had a way of filling a room—not with noise, but with warmth, like sunlight across a hardwood floor. She had a gentle steadiness about her, a grace that never faltered, even when life did.

She was not just the keeper of the house—she was the keeper of hearts. Her love did not arrive in big proclamations, but in fresh laundry, in biscuits baked from scratch, in prayers whispered beside the bed. She raised five children with hands that knew both work and tenderness, and a spirit that held us all together when the world did not.

And she was more than a mother—she was my closest friend. The one I could tell everything to. The one who knew me better than I knew myself. She held every story I was afraid to tell the world, and she did so with compassion, not judgment.

She raised us in the Methodist faith, rooted deep in scripture, hymns, and a humble reverence that shaped our days. We did not just go to church—we prepared for it. She would dress us in our Sunday best, make sure we were clean and pressed, not because of pride, but because of respect. I can still feel her straightening my collar, making sure we were ready—inside and out.

Throughout her life, she worked wherever she felt right . A canning factory, a shirt factory, stitching baseballs for Worth in Tullahoma—her hands always busy. She did whatever it took to take care of her family. No task was beneath her, and no job was too hard. There was purpose in everything she did.

Later in life, she took a brave step: she went back to school to become a nurse. She worried at first, unsure if she could do the coursework after so many years away from books and classrooms. But we stood by her. We helped when she stumbled. And she graduated. Walked across that threshold into a calling she was born for.

She worked at the Coffee County hospital, eventually caring for newborn babies—a job that was less a profession and more a fulfillment. After raising five of her own, she had a tenderness that could calm any cry. She loved that work deeply, and the work loved her back.

Even when her health began to decline, especially with bouts of pneumonia, she never lost her desire to be with family or with the past. We spent hours walking cemeteries together, tracing the names of ancestors, breathing history among the headstones. I remember one day at the McMinnville Library, she said quietly, "If I go down with it again, I don't think I'll make it." I did not want to believe it then.

But when she turned seventy, the illness came back. Stronger this time. It pulled her away, slowly, quietly, like a sunset that does not announce the night.

At the end, she was in a hospital in Nashville. I went to be with her—just the two of us. The room was hushed, but I swear her spirit waited for me. I sat beside her and prayed: "God, take my strength. Give it to her." I wanted her to stay. But heaven was calling, and this time, she answered.

She left with grace, the same way she lived. I still feel her with me—when I walk through a cemetery, when a hymn floats through the air, or when someone unexpected says, "I love you."

Because that was, her saying. "I love you." She gave it freely. To strangers, to family, to anyone who needed to hear it. It was not flirtation, it was conviction. It was Christ-like love, lived in practice. I picked it up from her, and I carry it now in my own voice. Sometimes it surprises people. But I say it anyway.

Because she taught me that if there is anything worth giving in this life, it is that.

*"She did not ask for legacy—she lived one. In every room she cleaned every child she comforted, and every soul she steadied, she left her mark. She clothed us not just in fabric, but in dignity, faith, and love.

I was there when she took her last breath—wrapped in love, not alone. And wherever memory holds her, I will be there too."*

The Adams Lineage – Roots of Grace and Grit

The Life and Spirit of Bessie Mae Brown

Born: May 15, 1911 – Cookeville, Putnam County, Tennessee Died: June 29, 1995 – Manchester, Coffee County, Tennessee Tags: Brown Family Line Asbury Roots Matriarchal Wisdom Faith and Fire

My grandmother, Bessie Mae Brown, was born in 1911 in Cookeville, Tennessee, at a time when the world was changing fast—but rural life still moved to the rhythm of land, family, and firewood-fed stoves. She came from people who worked with their hands and spoke their minds, and she carried that spirit with her whole life.

She was the daughter of Thomas Houston Brown Sr., a World War I veteran from Fayetteville, and Margaret Susan Peden, who was born at the small crossroads of

Daylight, Warren County. From them she inherited duty, strength, and just enough mischief to keep things lively.

Bessie eventually made her home in the Asbury community of Coffee County, including my mother, Helen Maxine Adams. Though her marriage to Aubrey Lee Adams ended in divorce, she helped raised Helen's children with determination and love—and no shortage of spunk.

She lived with us, and her presence was the kind you felt even before she walked in the room. She was always doing something to help folding laundry, offering a sharp opinion, minding the house, or hollering when the "youngins" got too far out of sight. That was her word for us: "Youngins!" She would call it out across the yard like a bell ringing time for supper—or mischief.

She never learned to drive, which meant I got to be her chauffeur. I would take her to visit Kinfolk, and the trip never ended where it started. She would say, "Let's just stop by so-and-so's," and next thing I knew, she was unpacked and staying there for a while. She was like that—always on the move when she felt the pull of kin. She may not have driven a car, but she steered her own life all the same.

She was a pistol in a house dress. Sharp-witted, loving, always ready to speak her mind and stand by her family. And while she might have fussed a little—"Youngins, get in this house!"—she was the first to defend us if we were ever corrected by someone else: "Now leave those young ins alone—I told them they could!"

Bessie passed away in 1995 in Manchester, but the fire she lit did not go out—it just got passed down. Her laughter echoes in family gatherings, her sayings still pop out in our voices, and the strength she carried shows up every time one of us faces the world with a little stubbornness, a lot of love, and no apologies. Bessie Mae Brown was more than a name on a family tree—she was the soft-spoken matriarch whose life rooted generations in strength, sacrifice, and

Southern grace. Her daughter, Helen Maxine Adams, carried her quiet endurance forward, and through Helen, a legacy of unity took shape—one 'K' name at a time. But before Helen, it was Bessie who tended the hearth, braided stories into daily life, and carved them out belonging in the hills of Coffee County.

> "She didn't raise her voice much—but she raised a daughter who became the heart of our home." > "She wasn't just from the Brown family—she was the reason the Brown spirit still runs strong in us today." 💍

Marriages: Bessie Mae Brown (1911–1995)

1st Husband: Aubrey Lee Adams 1915-1983

Birth: 12 November 1915 • Coffee County, Tennessee

Death: 12 October 1983 • Euclid, Cuyahoga County, Ohio

Marriage year: 1933 (documented)

Children: One daughter, Helen Maxine Adams

Aubrey was the father of Bessie's only child, Helen Maxine. Together they built a home rooted in kinship, passing down the Brown-Adams legacy that still flourishes today.

2nd Husband: Jesse Thurman Bryan 1892-1973

Birth: 12 September 1892 • Hillsboro, Coffee County, Tennessee

Death: 24 October 1973 • Manchester, Coffee County, Tennessee

Jesse was Bessie's second husband—a widower with deep ties to the Hillsboro community. Their bond was quiet, respectful, and companionate, bringing comfort later in Bessie's life.

3rd Husband: Robert L. McMahon 1907–1968

Birth: 20 November 1907 • Doyle, White County, Tennessee

Death: 7 April 1968 • Centertown, Warren County, Tennessee

Robert became Bessie's third husband after the passing of Jesse. A kind man with roots in Warren County, Robert's time with Bessie was brief yet meaningful—two lives intersecting with warmth and understanding during their final chapters.

🌳 *Thomas & Margaret: Foundation Beneath the Branches*

Thomas Houston Brown Sr.

Born: 29 July 1888 – Fayetteville, Lincoln County, Tennessee

Died: 2 November 1959 – Asbury, Coffee County, Tennessee

Margaret Susan Peden

Born: 11 November 1889 – Daylight, Warren County, Tennessee

Died: 16 June 1949 – Asbury, Coffee County, Tennessee

Thomas Houston Brown Sr. and his wife, Margaret Susan Peden. Thomas was born on July 29, 1888, in Fayetteville, Lincoln County, and Margaret on November 11, 1889, in the fittingly named town of Daylight, Warren County. Together, they built a life in Asbury, Coffee County—a place that would cradle their family's future.

Thomas passed on November 2, 1959, and Margaret on June 16, 1949. Their union was one of quiet strength and shared purpose. As the parents of Bessie Mae Brown and grandparents of Helen Maxine Adams, they were the unseen architects of a generational legacy—one rooted in perseverance, tenderness, and the rhythms of Southern life. Their hands tilled the land, folded Sunday linens, and steadied the shoulders of the next in line. Through them, a legacy of dignity and devotion found its form. *Children of Thomas Houston Brown Sr. & Margaret Susan Peden

Clara Ellen Brown 1909–1946 Birth: April 4, 1909, • Warren County, Tennessee Death: April 17, 1946, • Daylight Community, Warren County,

Tennessee Spouse: Colonel Cheatum Jones, 1905-1958

Bessie Mae Brown 1911–1995 Birth: May 15, 1911, • Cookeville, Putnam County, Tennessee Death: June 29, 1995, • Manchester, Coffee County, Tennessee Spouses: first: Aubery Lee Adams; 2nd Thurman Brayan; third: Robert McMahan

Harmon Chester Brown 1913–1989 Birth: May 3, 1913, • Warren County, Tennessee Death: September 27, 1989, • Warren County, Tennessee Spouse: Berchie Lou Pinegar, 1916-1974

Audy Iowa Brown 1915–1993 Birth: November 6, 1915, • Viola, Warren County, Tennessee Death: October 11, 1993, • Paducah, McCracken County, Kentucky Spouse: Marjorie Ethel Ashby, 1924-2005

Thomas Ambrose Brown Jr. 1918–1993 Birth: April 27, 1918, • Warren County, Tennessee Death: November 2, 1993, • Michigan City, Clinton County, Indiana Spouse: Thelma Jean Haggard, 1934-2018

Johnnie Brown 1920–1997 Birth: August 21, 1920, • Warren County, Tennessee Death: June 25, 1997, • Arlington, Dallas County, Texas Spouse: Reba Louise Kaylor, 1924-1992

Ruth Ann Brown 1922–1976 Birth: October 16, 1922, • Coffee County, Tennessee Death: January 25, 1976, • Palmer, Grundy County, Tennessee Spouse: William Bill Douglas Dishroon, 1920-1997

Robert E. Lee Brown 1933–1997 Birth June 10, 1933, • Viola, Coffee County, Tennessee Death: March 25, 1997, • McMinnville, Warren County, Tennessee Spouse: Imogene Smartt, 1934-2005 **Aubrey Lee Adams (1915–1983)**

Born: 12 November 1915, Coffee County, Tennessee Died: 12 October 1983, Euclid, Cuyahoga County, Ohio Buried: Chesterland, Geauga County, Ohio Military Service: United States Army, WWII (Enlisted 2 April 1943 in Cleveland, Ohio)

Aubrey Lee Adams was born in the heart of rural Tennessee to Robert Taylor Adams and Leta Neva Zumbro. His early life unfolded in the foothills of Coffee County during a time when America was still reeling from the Great War. In 1933, he married Bessie Mae Brown, and the following year they welcomed a daughter, **Helen Maxine Adams**, who later married into the Anderson family.

In 1941, Aubrey remarried—this time to **Emma Louise Lapp** in Cuyahoga County, Ohio. Just two years later, amid the storm of global conflict, he joined the U.S. Army. His enlistment on April 2, 1943, marked a defining chapter in his life. Like so many from his generation, he answered the call to serve with quiet determination.

Aubrey Lee Adams

Spouse 1: Bessie Mae Brown

Birth: 15 May 1911 • Cookeville, Putnam County, Tennessee, USA

Death: 29 June 1995 • Manchester, Coffee County, Tennessee, USA

Marriage: 5 August 1933 • Tennessee, USA

Child: Helen Maxine Adams (1934–2004)

Spouse 2: Emma Louise Lapp

Birth: 5 March 1911 • Jefferson County, Kentucky, USA

Death: 2 August 1991 • Euclid, Lake County, Ohio, USA

Marriage: 12 April 1941 • Cuyahoga County, Ohio, USA

The Legacy of Robert Taylor Adams & Leta Neva Zumbro

Robert Born: April 5, 1895 – Coffee County, Tennessee Died: December 17, 1966 – Coffee County, Tennessee Leta Born: August 11, 1897 – Hillsboro, Coffee County, Tennessee Died: April 5, 1980 – Ragsdale Road, Coffee County, Tennessee Tags: Adams Roots Zumbro Lineage Southern Soil Heritage Builders

Together, Robert and Leta Adams built their life—and legacy—in the quiet heart of Coffee County, Tennessee. They were born of that soil, married into it, and never strayed far from the hills that raised them.

Robert lived through eras of war, hardship, and slow Southern change, carrying the family name with quiet steadiness. Leta matched him with grace. She was born with a lyrical name and a strength forged over firewood and flour sacks. Their marriage produced more than children, it produced roots, the kind that hold generations steady.

Their home along Ragsdale Road was not grand, but it was a pillar. The front porch bore the weight of stories and summers, and the land carried laughter, labor, and memory. It was the kind of place where life was not always easy, but it was always real.

I used to ride my bike over to her house, down a gravel road so dusty it would leave a white film on my legs by the time I arrived. She did not have air conditioning—no one did—but when it got hot, she and her sister Berthe would sit on the porch, cutting quilt patterns and swapping kinfolk talk. They had married brothers—Leta wed Robert, Berthe married Andrew—and their bond was sewn as tightly as the quilts they made.

Sometimes I would be out in the grape vines, sneaking fruit, and get caught. They would call me to the porch with a grin and a lesson: "Sit and cut, then." Now, if you have never spent a summer day cutting quilt patterns, you do not know blistered fingers. That porch discipline hurt more than a spanking—and healed better too.

I would mow her yard, first with a heavy old push-blade mower that sang as it chopped, and later with a gas-powered one that still had to be pushed. She would joke and say, "Make sure you cut me a path to the privy!"—because there was no bathroom inside, just an outhouse out back. I did not just make her a path. I cut the whole yard like it was a baseball field—because I loved her, and that was how I showed it.

When the peddler came by on his old school bus, she would buy essential flour, thread—and sometimes a piece of bubble gum just for me. You did not get sweets every day back then. That one piece was a treasure.

And when she wanted a Coke, she would hand me some change and I would ride over to the store on Rock Road, pick up three glass bottles, and bring them back warm—and no one cared. That porch, those sisters, those quilts…that was a world of its own.

Their Children

Together, Robert and Leta raised a strong and steady family. Their children carried with them not just the Adams name, but the depth of character born on southern land and sewn into cotton quilts.

Aubrey Lee Adams

Birth: 12 November 1915 • Coffee County, Tennessee, USA

Death: 12 October 1983 • Euclid, Cuyahoga County, Ohio, USA

Spouse 1: Bessie Mae Brown

Birth: 15 May 1911 • Cookeville, Putnam County, Tennessee, USA

Death: 29 June 1995 • Manchester, Coffee County, Tennessee, USA

Marriage: 5 August 1933 • Tennessee, USA

Child: Helen Maxine Adams (1934–2004)

Spouse 2: Emma Louise Lapp

Birth: 5 March 1911 • Jefferson County, Kentucky, USA

Death: 2 August 1991 • Euclid, Lake County, Ohio, USA

Marriage: 12 April 1941 • Cuyahoga County, Ohio,

Gladys Marie Adams (1918–2011) Rooted in Hubbard's Cove, Tennessee. Her life was a long song of family, faith, and front porches.   Spouse: Claude C. Rhea

Birth: 22 November 1909 • Hubbard's Cove, Grundy County, Tennessee, USA

Death: 14 December 1992 • Warren County, Tennessee, USA

Marriage: 9 May 1937 • Grundy County, Tennessee, USA

Child: James Calvin Rhea (1938–2019)

Johnnie B. Adams (1926–2002) A quiet man who lived and passed in Coffee County. His loyalty ran deep—like the fields he knew. Spouse: Jessie Ruth Farrar

Birth: 1 May 1927 • Coffee County, Tennessee, USA

Death: 13 May 1988 • Coffee County, Tennessee, USA

Burial: Fredonia, Coffee County, Tennessee, USA

Marriage: 14 January 1946 • Tennessee,

Alma Jean Adams (1935–1935) A twin whose time on earth lasted only a day. But love claimed her place in the family forever.

Wilma Jean Adams(twin to Alma Jean) (1935–2012) Born with her sister and carried her memory every step. From Coffee County to Nashville, she moved with strength and softness.

Spouse: James Wendall Eaton

Birth: 2 April 1934 • Bedford County, Tennessee

Death: 19 December 2007 • Nashville, Davidson County, Tennessee

Burial: Nashville, Davidson County, Tennessee

> "Sometimes, when I think back, I miss them so. Not for moments or milestones but for the feel of warm Coke bottles, the smell of grape jam, the sound of scissors on quilt scraps, and the gravel road that brought me to everything I loved."

The Land and the Legacy — Henry's Cove and Its People

To understand the Anderson family is to understand the land they call home. No place defines that connection more fully than **Henry's Cove**, *nestled at the base of the* **Cumberland Mountain** *in* **Coffee County, Tennessee**. *More than just a geographic feature, Henry's Cove is a living memory, a cradle of kinship, and the stage upon which much of your family's story has played out.*

Named after **Samuel Houston Henry**, a man connected by blood to the patriot **Patrick Henry**, the cove stands as a quiet symbol of resilience and settlement. Its forests, creeks, and fertile bottomland have nourished generations. It was here that **Capt. John Watson Anderson** made his home, while surveying the county line that would divide **Coffee** from **Grundy County**, tracing it along the **mountain's rugged spine**.

Though he worked the high ridgelines and measured the border between counties, John chose to live below—in the green valley that offered shelter, fresh water, and room to farm and raise a family. He taught school, led men into the Mexican War, and performed county clerk duties, but always returned to Henry's Cove. John married Sarah Darnell and together they raised a large family steeped in tradition and rooted in place. The soil there held not only crops, but memory.

His son, **Nathaniel Hamilton Anderson**, married **Sally Adelaide Horton**, and together they carried forward the values of service and endurance. Their son, **Edgar Anderson**, married Harriet E. Jones, a woman whose strength matched the hard years they faced after Reconstruction. They built a life in Hillsboro, farming and raising children in the quiet strength of community. It was said that they fought over their snuff cans a lot. LOL!!

Their son, Abb Anderson, married Willie Jane Phillips (1908-1991), born 30 March 1908 in Hillsboro, Coffee County, Tennessee, and passed away 13 October 1991 in Manchester, Coffee County, Tennessee. Willie Jane was the daughter of Robert Calvin Phillips (1881-1942), born 22 August 1881 in Hillsboro, Coffee County, Tennessee, and passed away 8 March 1942 in Hillsboro, Coffee County, Tennessee. Robert Calvin Phillips was the son of William Abraham Phillips (1856-1926), born 1 September 1856 in Hillsboro, Coffee County, Tennessee, and passed away 16 March 1926 in Hillsboro. . William Abraham was the son of George Washington Phillips (1833-1915), born 21 December 1833 in Emanuel County, Georgia, and died 1 August 1915 in Hillsboro, Coffee County, Tennessee. George Washington was the son of James Farris Phillips (1804-1889), born 28 March 1804 in Amherst County, Virginia, and died 24 December 1889 in Hillsboro, Coffee County, Tennessee. James Farris was the son of Johnson Phillips (1772-1847), born 14 August 1772 in Amherst County, Virginia, and died 26 December 1847 in Hillsboro, Coffee County, Tennessee. Johnson was the son of John Phillips (1742-1795), born 28 May 1742 in Orange County, Virginia, and died in 1795 in Amherst County, Virginia. John Phillips was the son of Joseph Phillips (1710-1774), born in 1710 in England, and died in 1774 in Surry County, North Carolina. Joseph was the son of William Phillips (1688-1739), born in 1688 in North Farnham Parish, Richmond, Virginia, and died in 1739 in Virginia. William was the son of William Phillips **(1640-1725)**, born **12 July 1640** in **Newport, Newport County, Rhode Island**, and died **December 1725** in **Newport, Rhode Island**. William was the son of **Richard Phillips (1594-?)**, born **19 May 1594** in **Sutton Maddock, Shropshire, England**. Richard was the son of **Richard Phillips (1550-?)**, born **4 January 1550** in **Pontesbury, Shropshire, England**. Richard was the son of **John Phillips (1502-1551)**, born **in 1502** in **Picton Castle, Pembroke, Wales**, and died **in 1551** in **Picton Castle, Pembroke, Wales**. John was the son of **Thomas Phillips (1456-1550)**, born **in 1456** in **Cilsant Castle, St Clears**

Dyfed, Carmarthenshire, Wales, and died in 1550 in Castlebythe, Pembroke, Wales. Thomas was the son of **Philip Phillips (1415-1441)**, born in 1415 in **Cilsant Castle, St Clears Dyfed, Carmarthenshire, Wales**, and died in 1441 in **Cilsant, Wales**. Philip was the son of **Maredudd Phillips (1382-?)**, born in 1382 in **Cilsant, Sir, Lord of Cilsant, Wales**, and died in **Cilsant, Wales**. Maredudd was the son of **Llwc Llawen Phillip (1344-?)**, born in 1344 in **Cilsant, St Clears Dyfed, Carmarthenshire, Wales**, and died in **Cilsant, Wales**. Willie Jane was a devoted wife and mother who helped steer the family through the Great Depression and into the modern era.

In **1932**, their son, **Robert Kenneth Anderson Sr.**, was born. He would later marry **Helen Maxine Adams (1934-2004)**, born **29 May 1934** in **Hillsboro, Coffee County, Tennessee**, and passed away **28 September 2004** in **Nashville, Davidson County, Tennessee**, a woman whose own roots run deep in the Tennessee soil. Helen came from the **Adams family**, long settled in southern Tennessee, with ancestral ties to early settlers in Warren and Grundy Counties. Her father, **Aubrey Lee Adams (1915-1983)**, born **12 November 1915** in **Coffee County, Tennessee**, and passed away **12 October 1983** in **Euclid, Cuyahoga County, Ohio**, and her mother, **Sarah Louella Gilliam**, both came from farming families who worked the same soil, worshipped in the same country churches, and endured the same struggles as the Andersons.

Aubrey Lee Adams was the son of **Robert Taylor Adams (1895-1966)**, born **5 April 1895** in Viola, Warren **County, Tennessee**, and died **17 December 1966** Ragsdale, Coffee County, Tennessee. Robert Taylor was the son of **Benjamin Harrison Adams Jr. (1860-1932)**, born **21 December 1860** in **Coffee County, Tennessee**, and passed away **12 October 1932** in **Monteagle, Grundy County, Tennessee**. Benjamin Jr. was the son of **Benjamin Harrison Adams Sr. (1820-1898)**, born **4 June 1820** in **Viola, Warren**

County, Tennessee, and passed away **9 December 1898** in **Stick, Coffee County, Tennessee**. Benjamin Sr. was the son of **John Adams (1791-1860)**, born **27 September 1791** in **Mountain Creek, Lincoln County, North Carolina**, and passed away around **1860** in **Stick, Coffee County, Tennessee**. John Adams was the son of **Elijah Adams (1766-1850)**, born **12 February 1766** in **Rowan County, North Carolina**, and died **19 April 1850** in **Macon County, Tennessee**.

Abb and Willie Jane Phillps Anderson

Abb Anderson (1906–1978)

"The Grit in the Grain"

Born into a new century and shaped by hardship, **Abb Anderson** was the kind of man who did not speak often—but when he did, his words were remembered. By the time the Great Depression swept through rural Tennessee, he had already learned that life rarely gave second chances, so he did not waste first ones. With calloused hands and quiet faith, Abb planted, ran, and brought potatoes, repaired, endured. Every fence post he set and prayer he whispered deepened the grooves of a legacy carved from necessity and loyalty.

He married Willie Jane Phillips and together they built a home that survived not by comfort, but by rhythm—planting in spring, storing in summer, stitching, and sacrificing come fall. Abb's work boots never quite wore out, and neither did the respect he earned across the years—from church pews, tractor seats, and dinner tables alike. His laugh rumbled like a tractor engine, and his silence could speak more than sermons. "He likes to go and barter for things they need."

To his children, he was both a lighthouse and load-bearer. To his descendants, he is proof that perseverance leaves fingerprints deeper than fame.

Anderson Branch – Weathered and Woven

The Steadfast Life of Abb Anderson

Born: February 26, 1902 – Hillsboro, Coffee County, Tennessee Died: November 8, 1951 – Hillsboro, Coffee County, Tennessee Tags: Anderson Patriarch Hillsboro Roots Life of the Land Legacy Connector

Born at the turn of a new century, Abb Anderson spent his life cradled in the ridges and red soil of Hillsboro, Coffee County. Whether farming, raising children, or carving out a life alongside his wife Willie Jane, he was a man of few words and firm purpose.

Abb died young—just 49 years old—taken too soon by cancer. His grandchildren never knew his handshake, but they carry pieces of his name, his strength, and his silence.

> "He was not just from Hillsboro—he was Hillsboro. In his handshake, his hat brim, and the way he carried silence like a trusted friend.

The Enduring Grace of Willie Jane Phillips Anderson

Born: March 30, 1908 – Hillsboro, Coffee County, Tennessee Died: October 13, 1991 – Hillsboro, Coffee County, Tennessee Spouse: Abb Anderson (1902–1951) Tags: Phillips Family Anderson Matriarch Gold Star Mother Hillsboro & Manchester Caretaker Legacy

Willie Jane was raised in Hillsboro and spent all her life there—except the years after Abb's death, when she moved to Manchester and opened her heart and home to boarders in need. She cooked their meals, provided them shelter, and gave them something more than room and board: a place to belong.

She was also a Gold Star Mother, having lost her son James Dewey Anderson in WWII. It was a private grief she carried with dignity and prayer.

> "She outlived her husband, her son, and so many seasons. But through it all, she stayed strong—and she stayed kind."

To her grandson, Brian, she was presence and peace:

> "I mowed her yard as a boy. She would watch from the porch and smile—a kind of porchlight love you could carry through your whole life. She was not just family. She was presence."

Children of Abb Anderson & Willie Jane Phillips

All born in Coffee County, Tennessee.

1. **James Dewey Anderson** – Killed in action during World War IIus > Gold Star Son – a silent sacrifice carried in his mother's eyes.

Spouse: Eva Mae Owen

Birth: 8 October 1926 • Cannon County, Tennessee

Death: 1 November 2011 • Manchester, Coffee County, Tennessee

2. **Lora Virginia Anderson** (1929–2006) – Manchester, TN > The bridge between old Hillsboro and a new century. Quiet grace, enduring love.

Spouse: Billy Steven Moore

Birth: 29 February 1927 • Harvey, Lincoln County, Illinois

Death: 9 September 1996 • Manchester, Coffee County, Tennessee

3. **Robert Kenneth Anderson Sr**. (1932–2015) – Hillsboro, TN > A man of quiet strength, a lifelong son of Hillsboro—and a father remembered daily by his son, Brian. > "He was my father, and I miss him. But every name I record, every root I trace, carries part of him forward.

Spouse: Helen Maxine Adams

Birth: 29 May 1934 • Hillsboro, Coffee County, Tennessee

Death: 28 September 2004 • Nashville, Davidson County, Tennessee

4. **Donald Eugene Anderson Sr.** (1934–2013) – Manchester, TN > A soft-spoken landmark—Uncle Donald stood like a fencepost in family soil.

Spouse: Cleta May Chambers

Birth: 8 May 1935 • Langston, Jackson County, Alabama

Death: 17 November 2011 • Manchester, Coffee County, Tennessee

Shirley Faye Anderson (1939–2015) – Beech Grove, TN > Aunt Shirley's joy was she was a pistol. Spouse: Jimmy Wendall Driver

   Birth: 31 March 1939 • Beech Grove, Coffee County, Tennessee

   Death: Feb 8, 2015, Beech Grove, Coffee County, Tennessee

> "From the Hillsboro earth they rose, seven roots weathered by sorrow, strength, and time. Some stayed. Some served. Some watched. But all of them built something lasting. And through the pages of this book, they live again."

Spouse: Willie Jane Phillips

Birth: 30 March 1908 • Hillsboro, Coffee County, Tennessee

Death: 13 October 1991 • Hillsboro, Coffee County, Tennessee

Gold Star Mothers, Willie Jane Phillips Anderson

Voices from the Ridge: A Family's Journey Through Time

by

Brian Keith Anderson Volume I:

The Phillips, Poff & Anderson Lines

Chapter Six

The Anderson Legacy – Carried by Grace and Grit

Willie Jane Phillips Anderson Born March 30, 1908 – Hillsboro, Tennessee Died October 13, 1991 – Hillsboro, Tennessee

She was the kind of woman who did not need to say much to be heard. When Abb Anderson passed too young, she did not fold. She opened her doors in Manchester to boarders, turned recipes into survival, and carried the weight of grief with a grace that stretched across generations. She was a mother, a widow, and a Gold Star.

> "She did not just survive. She held us together. And somehow, she always had enough strength for everyone but herself.

The Phillips Line – Roots Beneath the Ridge

Robert Calvin PhillipsBorn August 22, 1881 – Hillsboro, TN Died March 8, 1942 – Hillsboro, TN

Gracie Ann Poff Phillips Born May 10, 1883 – Hillsboro, TN Died October 10, 1948 – Hillsboro, TN

Together, they raised eight children in Hillsboro—a town stitched into red clay and tobacco dust. They did not make headlines. They made legacies: in gardens, in prayer books, in the way their children stayed close.

> "Not all legacies are loud. Some are made of woodsmoke, calloused hands, and the silent pride of a father and mother who never left home."

Children of Robert Calvin & Gracie Ann Phillips:

Dillard Frank Phillips

Born: July 28, 1897 – Hillsboro, Coffee County, Tennessee   Died: July 23, 1979 – Scott County, Tennessee

Spouse: Elsie Martha Chambers

Born: March 30, 1904 – Scott County, Tennessee   Died: July 23, 1986 – Scott County

Ernest W. Phillips

Born: November 6, 1904 – Tennessee   Died: July 5, 1968 – Hillsboro, Coffee County, Tennessee

Spouse: Ethel Bradie Basham

Born: April 25, 1908 – Hillsboro, Coffee County, Tennessee   Died: February 3, 2000 – Hillsboro, Coffee County, Tennessee

Willie Jane Phillips

Born: March 30, 1908 – Hillsboro, Coffee County, Tennessee 🕊Died: October 13, 1991 – Hillsboro, Coffee County, Tennessee

Spouse; Abb Anderson

Born: February 26, 1902 – Hillsboro, Coffee County, Tennessee   Died: November 8, 1951 – Hillsboro, Coffee County, Tennessee

Lora Mae Phillips

Born: September 3, 1910 – Hillsboro, Coffee County, Tennessee   Died: November 24, 1995 – Owens Crossroads, Madison County, Alabama

Spouse: William F. Pylant

Born: April 29, 1903 – Hurricane, Madison County, Alabama Died: June 18, 1985 – Madison, Madison County, Alabama

Jessie D. Phillips

Born: November 4, 1914 – Hillsboro, Coffee County, Tennessee   Died: July 8, 1930 – Hillsboro, Coffee County, Tennessee

Mary P. Phillips

Born: August 21, 1919 – Hillsboro, Coffee County, Tennessee   Died: January 9, 1981 – Hillsboro, Coffee County, Tennessee

Spouse: Sanford Kennedy

Born: April 28, 1914 – Tennessee, USA   Died: April 29, 1970 – Hillsboro, Coffee County, Tennessee

Bobie Lee Phillips

Born: October 26, 1923 – Coffee County, Tennessee   Died: January 26, 1924 – Hillsboro, Coffee County, Tennessee

Linage of Robert Calvin Phillips

The **Robert Calvin Phillips** in your manuscript is the one born in 1881 in Hillsboro, Tennessee. He is:

The **father of Willie Jane Phillips**, who married Abb Anderson.

The **grandfather of Robert Kenneth Anderson Sr.**, and great-grandfather to you.

Part of a deep Tennessee-rooted Phillips line that traces back to **George Washington Phillips**, James Farris Phillips, and to John Phillips (1742–1795) and beyond.

1. The Poff Legacy – Woven from Quiet Strength

James Marshall Poff Born December 22, 1855 – Limestone County, AL Died October 15, 1943 – Limestone County, AL

Harriet Julye McNuttBorn July 26, 1858 – Bedford County, TN Died July 25, 1887 – Bedford County, TN

James and Harriet lived through war, plague, and hardship. She died young. He lived long enough to see their children grow and the world remade more than once.

> "She bore eight lives in eight years. He buried her, then raised them. This is what love looks like when time does not make it easy."

Minnie Etta Poff

Born: July 1, 1879 – Bedford County, Tennessee   Died: May 6, 1959 – Tullahoma, Coffee County, Tennessee

Spouse: John D. Martin

Born: Circa 1868 – Tennessee

   Died: Date unknown – Tullahoma, Coffee County, Tennessee

Dessie Lee Poff

Born: October 15, 1880 – Hillsboro, Coffee County, Tennessee   Died: November 20, 1967 – Nashville, Davidson County, Tennessee

Spouse: Isaac Newton Waller

Born: December 12, 1878 – Alabama   Died: March 25, 1955 – Nashville, Davidson County, Tennessee

Gracie Ann Poff

Born: May 10, 1883 – Hillsboro, Coffee County, Tennessee

   Died: October 10, 1948 – Hillsboro, Coffee County, Tennessee

Spouse: Robert Calvin Phillips

Born: August 22, 1881 – Hillsboro, Coffee County, Tennessee

   Died: March 8, 1942 – Hillsboro, Coffee County, Tennessee, James Oliver Poff

Born: April 27, 1885 – Bedford County, Tennessee

Lulu May Poff

Born: July 10, 1887 – Bedford County, Tennessee

Died: July 23, 1887 – Bedford County, Tennessee

Trudie Ethel Poff

Born: August 8, 1891 – Manchester, Coffee County, Tennessee

Died: March 29, 1970 – Athens, Limestone County, Alabama

Spouse: Carlos Edward Chambers

Born: January 17, 1889 – Coxey Community, Limestone County, Alabama

Died: January 26, 1968 – Coxey Community, Limestone County, Alabama

Kenneth, Virginia, Donald, Shirley, Baba (Willie Jane in Chair)

🏛 *Edgar Anderson and Harriet Jones Anderson*

"The Gentleman Farmer"

Edgar Anderson straddled two eras—one rooted in hand-hewn timber and the other inching toward modern machinery. Born in the post-Reconstruction South, he witnessed the country's heartland shift from candles to kerosene, from spoken prayer to printed promise. Through it all, Edgar remained faithful to the land, his family, and the deeply held belief that integrity was man's most valuable crop.

He was a man of contradiction—soft-spoken but resolute, traditional yet quietly curious. His seed catalogues carried penciled notes in the margins, not just calculations but verses, musings, and little poems written between fence mending and harvests. His fields were not just rows of corn and cotton; they were rows of intention—proof that labor, when done with love, could be a form of prayer.

Edgar married **Harriet E. Jones**, a woman whose strength matched his, though hers was worn in the kitchen and sung in lullabies. Together, they raised a generation shaped by both hymn and hoe. He taught his children to speak plainly and work patiently. His boots were always polished, even when covered in dust—because dignity, for Edgar, lived not in appearance but in preparation.

When he passed in 1955, the family did not just lose a provider. They lost a compass—quiet but unwavering. And today, with every story we tell, every prayer we whisper over supper, his voice walks beside us still.

Edgar Anderson (1871–1956)

Born: January 30, 1871 – Hillsboro, Coffee County, Tennessee **Died:** February 4, 1956 – Hillsboro, Coffee County, Tennessee **Burial:** Coffee County, Tennessee, United States

🌿 Family

Parents: Nathaniel Hamilton Anderson (1845–1919) & Sally Adelaide Horton (1844–1917)

Siblings: William H., Edward, Virginia Pearl, Luther Nathaniel, John Watson

Spouse: Harriet E. Jones (1873–1967), married August 26, 1893

Children:

David Andrew Anderson

Born: January 16, 1894 – Indian Territory, Oklahoma

Died: June 24, 1975 – Southfield, Oakland County, Michigan

Spouse: Annie Elizabeth Caldwell

Born: September 11, 1895 – Grundy County, Tennessee

Died: March 10, 1978 – Livonia, Wayne County, Michigan

Leonard "Pete" Wood Anderson

Born: April 21, 1896 – Hillsboro, Coffee County, Tennessee

Died: October 17, 1960 – Hillsboro, Coffee County, Tennessee

Spouse: Hazel Uselton

Born: July 28, 1901 – Tennessee

Died: June 25, 1996 – Coffee County, Tennessee

George Dewey Anderson

Born: May 13, 1898 – Hillsboro, Coffee County, Tennessee

Died: May 14, 1980 – Hillsboro, Coffee County, Tennessee

Spouse: Arie Pauline Anderson

Born: June 24, 1908 – Beech grove, Coffee County, Tennessee

Died: July 8, 1994 – Manchester, Coffee County, Tennessee

Eva A. Anderson

Born: August 22, 1900 – Hillsboro, Coffee County, Tennessee

Died: March 29, 1985 – Hillsboro, Coffee County, Tennessee

Spouse: Marvin Price Jernigan Sr.

Born: September 29, 1887 – Coffee County, Tennessee

Died: October 28, 1939 – Hillsboro, Coffee County, Tennessee

Abb Anderson

Born: February 26, 1902 – Hillsboro, Coffee County, Tennessee

Died: November 8, 1951 – Hillsboro, Coffee County, Tennessee

Spouse: Willie Jane Phillips

Born: March 30, 1908 – Hillsboro, Coffee County, Tennessee

Died: October 13, 1991 – Hillsboro, Coffee County, Tennessee

Albert Anderson

Born: February 26, 1902 – Hillsboro, Coffee County, Tennessee

Died: February 7, 1985 – Hillsboro, Coffee County, Tennessee

Spouse: Hassie Ethel Enos

Born: July 30, 1907 – Woodbury, Cannon County, Tennessee

Died: December 12, 1994 – Hillsboro, Coffee County, Tennessee

Residences

Harriet E. Jones (1873–1967)

Born: March 11, 1873 – Hillsboro, Coffee County, Tennessee **Died:** June 22, 1967 – Hillsboro, Coffee County, Tennessee **Burial:** Coffee County, Tennessee, United States

Family

Parents James Armstrong Jones

Born: April 20, 1850 – Bradyville, Cannon County, Tennessee   Died: December 6, 1945 – Hillsboro, Coffee County, Tennessee   Relation: Your 2nd great-grandfather; father of Harriet E. Jones (1873-1967)   Parents: William Gilbert Jones (1816-1887) & Nancy Eleanor Roddey (1819-1888)   Marriages:

Emeline Jane Lay (1839-1926) – m. 1859, 1871, 1874, and 1887 (multiple records suggest symbolic or repeated unions)

Sarah Ann Reed (1854-1926) – m. August 12, 1871, Coffee County, TN (your direct ancestor)

Alie Jones (b. 1856) – m. 1877

Harriet E. Jones

Born: March 11, 1873 – Hillsboro, Coffee County, Tennessee

Died: June 22, 1967 – Hillsboro, Coffee County, Tennessee

Spouse: Edgar Anderson

Born: January 30, 1871 – Hillsboro, Coffee County, Tennessee

Died: February 4, 1956 –Hillsboro, Coffee County, Tennessee

John R. Jones

Born: October 21, 1875 – Hillsboro, Coffee County, Tennessee

Died: November 24, 1901 – Pike County, Kentucky

Spouse: Malissa Jane Smith

Born: February 1872 – Kentucky, USA

Died: August 17, 1912 – Pike County, Kentucky

Charles A. Jones

Born: 1876 – Hillsboro, Coffee County, Tennessee

Died: February 3, 1910 – Tennessee

Sally Jane Jones

Born: November 12, 1877 – Hillsboro, Coffee County, Tennessee

Died: July 28, 1909 – Tennessee

Lucy L. Jones

Born: About 1879 – Lonoke, Lonoke County, Arkansas, USA

Died: Unknown

James Lee Jones

Born: April 17, 1880 – Hillsboro, Coffee County, Tennessee

Died: July 16, 1963 – Hillsboro, Coffee County, Tennessee

Martha Ellen Jones

Born: August 27, 1882 – Manchester, Coffee County, Tennessee

Died: May 23, 1969 – Nashville, Davidson County, Tennessee

Spouse: James Hillary Brooks

Born: October 30, 1869 – Tennessee, USA

Died: March 5, 1935 – Manchester, Coffee County, Tennessee

Grover Cleveland Jones

Born: February 14, 1885 – Hillsboro, Coffee County, Tennessee

Died: January 20, 1971 – Tullahoma, Coffee County, Tennessee

Spouse: Louie Ellen Smith

Born: April 27, 1880 – Tennessee, USA

Died: September 1, 1957 – Hillsboro, Coffee County, Tennessee

Lovie Jane Jones

Born: September 25, 1888 – Hillsboro, Coffee County, Tennessee

Died: April 6, 1975 – Barbourville, Knox County, Kentucky

Spouse: Boger Earl Smith

Born: October 7, 1883 – Canada, Pike County, Kentucky, USA

Died: July 28, 1977 – Barbourville, Knox County, Kentucky

Ethel Meade Jones

Born: March 19, 1890 – Hillsboro, Coffee County, Tennessee

Died: January 19, 1914 – Hillsboro, Coffee County, Tennessee

Spouse: Andrew Ranson England

Born: May 22, 1886 – Hillsboro, Coffee County, Tennessee

Died: May 29, 1942 – Chattanooga, Hamilton County, Tennessee

Ida Mae Jones

Born: May 7, 1892 – Hillsboro, Coffee County, Tennessee

Died: Before 1920 – Coffee County, Tennessee

Spouse: Henry Whitmore "Whit" Dillingham

Born: October 12, 1887 – Bedford County, Tennessee

Died: January 20, 1919 – Coffee County, Tennessee

⚖️ Nathaniel Hamilton Anderson (1837–1909)

"The Civil Son"

Born just as Tennessee's hills were beginning to echo with industry and expansion, Nathaniel Hamilton Anderson came of age in a world simmering with contradiction. A teenager at the first whisper of secession, he was thrust into adulthood by the eruption of Civil War. He left home with boots too large and ideals too fragile, and when he returned, neither fit the same again.

Whether he carried a rifle or simply bore witness is not known in full, but what is certain is this: Nathaniel endured. The world he returned to was cracked—not just in its fences, but in its family bonds, its trust, its land. And so, he rebuilt—not with noise or glory, but with cedar rails and patient hands. He tended not only to soil, but to sons, not only wounds, but ways forward.

He married into a time of reconstruction, both literal and emotional. His legacy was not tallied in acres or medals, but in the hush of evenings when children rested safe, in the smell of corn rising on Sabbath mornings, in the silent dignity of a man who no longer spoke of the fire—but carried its ashes with grace.

Though his story lies beneath the stories of his descendants, Nathaniel's chapter is the hinge—between hardship and healing, division, and devotion. And in every quiet act of fatherhood, stewardship, or restraint, he wrote lines into the foundation of what would become the Anderson legacy.

⍰ Nathaniel Hamilton Anderson (1845–1919)

Born: June 18, 1845 – Hillsboro, Coffee County, Tennessee Died: May 8, 1919 – Hillsboro, Coffee County, Tennessee Burial: Hillsboro Presbyterian Church Cemetery, Coffee County, TN

🦴 Family

Parents: John Watson Anderson (1806–1879) & Sarah Jane Darnell (1811–1880)

Siblings: Elizabeth, Florence Jane, Sally, Alexander Peter, Virginia, James W., Andrew Lewis, Orlena, Sinah L.

Spouse: Sally Adelaide Horton (1844–1917), married April 19, 1869

Children:

William H. Anderson (1870–1922)

Born: March 12, 1870 – Hillsboro, Coffee County, Tennessee

Died: July 11, 1922 – Norman, Cleveland County, Oklahoma

Spouse: Hattie Lavenia Wilson (1869–1936)

Born: April 8, 1869 – Hillsboro, Coffee County, Tennessee Died: January 21, 1936 – Norman, Cleveland County, Oklahoma

Edgar Anderson (1871–1956)

Born: January 30, 1871 – Hillsboro, Coffee County, Tennessee

Died: February 4, 1956 – Hillsboro, Coffee County, Tennessee

Spouse: Harriet E. Jones (1873–1967)

Born: March 11, 1873 – Hillsboro, Coffee County, Tennessee

Died: June 22, 1967 – Hillsboro, Coffee County, Tennessee

Edward Anderson (1871–1929)

Born: January 30, 1871 – Hillsboro, Coffee County, Tennessee

Died: November 5, 1929 – Hillsboro, Coffee County, Tennessee

Spouse: Mary Ethel Smythe (1886–1967)

Born: August 31, 1886 – Coffee County, Tennessee Died: May 14, 1967 – Manchester, Coffee County, Tennessee Relationship: Wife of

❉ Virginia Pearl Anderson (1874–1910)

Born: October 1874 – Hillsboro, Coffee County, Tennessee

Died: February 26, 1910 – Tennessee

🛡 Spouse: Charlie Pratt (1876–1954)

Born: December 26, 1876 – Hillsboro, Coffee County, Tennessee

Died: November 28, 1954 – Hillsboro, Coffee County, Tennessee

❉ Luther Nathaniel Anderson (1877–1945)

Born: August 23, 1877 – Hillsboro, Coffee County, Tennessee

Died: May 8, 1945 – McMinnville, Warren County, Tennessee

🛡 Spouse: Joseph (Joe) Albert Lusk (1880–1970)

Born: October 3, 1880 – Hillsboro, Coffee County, Tennessee

Died: April 15, 1970 – Cannon County, Tennessee

❉ John Watson Anderson (1884–1961)

Born: January 10, 1884 – Hillsboro, Coffee County, Tennessee

Died: May 2, 1961 – Hollister, San Benito County, California

🛡 Spouse: Minnie May Bryan (1888–1967)

Born: May 1, 1888 – Hillsboro, Coffee County, Tennessee

Died: March 8, 1967 – Hollister, San Benito County, California

Wife: Sally Adelaide Horton (1844–1917)

Born: November 4, 1844 – Coffee County, Tennessee Died: April 5, 1917 – Hillsboro, Coffee County, Tennessee Burial: April 6, 1917 – Hillsboro, Tennessee

Family

Parents: John Mann Horton (1816-1893) & Sarah Ann Hensley (1814-1890)

Siblings: Emaline A., Jane, Henry Calvin, Mary Amelia, Vallien, William, Jessie, Joshua Film

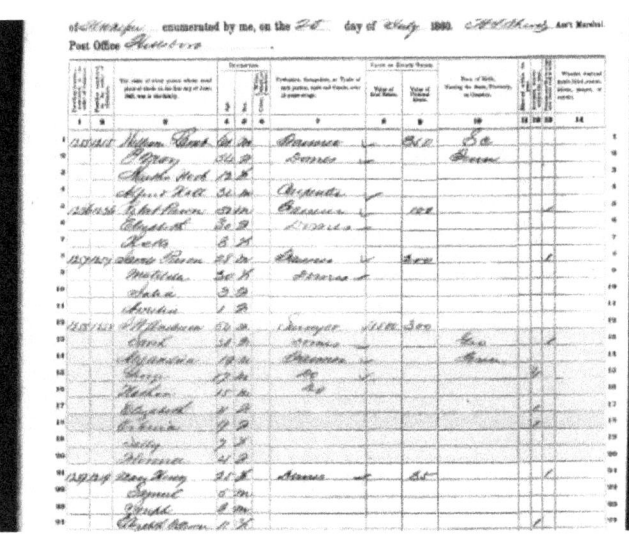

John Watson Anderson (1797-1879)

"The Horseman of the Ridge"

They say John Watson Anderson could read a trail like a scripture and tell the weather by the twitch of his mule's ear. Born in the final years of the 18th century—when Tennessee was still wrangling with its own identity, John was raised in a world where land meant legacy, and a man's word traveled farther than his voice.

His life was shaped by rhythm: sunrise, livestock, weather, and worship. With rough-hewn boots and a rider's posture, John moved through the ridge country not with arrogance, but with respect—for the land, the Lord, and the quiet knowledge passed down from his father, Peter Anderson, a Revolutionary War generation man whose presence still lingered like pipe smoke in the family cabin.

John kept a journal—simple, leather-bound, weathered at the seams. Its pages held more than births and barter records; they echoed daily reckonings: storms survived, horses traded, neighbors helped. These were not just facts. They were reflections, small markers that a man had lived well, done right, and believed in something beyond himself.

Though his world was modest, the scale of his influence stretched far beyond the boundaries of his fields. He raised children who carried his steadiness, his reverence, and his sense of duty into a new century. And in your blood, Brian—steady, thoughtful, devoted—his legacy gallops still.

❧❧❧ John Watson Anderson (1806–1879)

Born: March 25, 1806 - Franklin County, Tennessee, United States Died: December 27, 1879 - Hillsboro, Coffee County, Tennessee Burial: In Coffee County, Tennessee (exact cemetery unconfirmed)

🌿 Family

Parents: Peter Anderson Sr. (1765-1824) & Sinai Cynthia Roberts (1781-1874)

Siblings: Peter Jr., Edward Frost, William C., Cornelious Robert Benton, Andrew Berry, Catherine, and others

Spouse: Sarah Jane Darnell (1811-1880), married October 30, 1834, in Stokes County, North Carolina

Children:

❀ Virginia Anderson (1831–1881)

Born: 1831 - Jackson County, Alabama

Died: February 14, 1881 - St. Louis Ward 1, Saint Louis City, Missouri

💗 Spouse: William Potts (1827–bef. 1876) CSA

Born: 1827 - Tennessee,

Died: Before 1876 - St. Louis, Missouri, USA Relationship:

❀ Andrew Lewis Anderson (1833–1900)

Born: 1833 - Cowan, Franklin County, Tennessee

Died: 1900 - Rhea County, Tennessee, USA

Spouse: Unknown

❀ Sinah L. Anderson (1835–1914)

Born: March 25, 1835 - Jackson County, Alabama

Died: January 17, 1914 – Roff Town, Pontotoc County, Oklahoma Relationship: second

💜 First Spouse: Joseph Anderson (1835–1872)

Born: March 25, 1835 – Hackberry Bottoms, Roane County, Tennessee Died: May 7, 1872 – Tullahoma, Coffee County, Tennessee

💜 Second Spouse: John Edward Good Sr. (1810–1880)

Born: 1810 – North Carolina, USA Died: 1880 – Roff Town, Pontotoc County, Oklahoma

❉ Samuel Anderson (1837–Unknown)

Born: 1837 – Cowan, Franklin County, Tennessee

Died: Unknown

❉ James W. Anderson (1839–1900) CSA

Born: May 10, 1839 – Hillsboro, Coffee County, Tennessee

Died: 1900 – Pryor burg, Graves County, Kentucky

💜 Spouse: Sarah Jane Waggoner (1842–1915)

Born: April 11, 1842 – Knox County, Tennessee

Died: February 25, 1915 – Wingo, Graves County, Kentucky

❉ Alexander Peter Anderson (1841–1880) CSA

Born: 1841 – Hillsboro, Coffee County, Tennessee

Died: May 9, 1880 – Hillsboro, Coffee County, Tennessee

💗 Spouse: Mary Frances Gleeson (1835–1906)

Born: March 1835 – Madison, Madison County, Illinois, USA

Died: December 1906 – Navarro County, Texas, Second Husband: Franklin Shackleford (1834–1865)

✤ George W. Anderson (1843–Unknown) CSA

Born: May 13, 1843 – Hillsboro, Coffee County, Tennessee, USA

Died: Unknown – Last known residence in Tennessee

💗 Spouse: Louisa Setliff (1839–Unknown)

Born: 1839 – Mt. Airy, Surry County, North Carolina, USA

Died: Unknown – Last known residence in Tennessee

✤ Orlenia Anderson (1844–1908)

Born: July 1844 – Hillsboro, Coffee County, Tennessee, USA

Died: November 9, 1908 – Tennessee

💗 Spouse: Hillary Richard Winton (1834–1908)

Born: July 11, 1834 – Hillsboro, Coffee County, Tennessee, USA

Died: December 6, 1908 – Hillsboro, Coffee County, Tennessee, USA

✤ Nathaniel Hamilton Anderson (1845–1919) CSA

Born: June 18, 1845 – Hillsboro, Coffee County, Tennessee, USA

Died: May 8, 1919 – Hillsboro, Coffee County, Tennessee,

Second Wife: Julia C. Kimsey (1844–1925)

💛Sally Adelaide Horton (1844–1917)

Born: November 4, 1844 – Coffee County, Tennessee, USA

Died: April 5, 1917 – Hillsboro, Coffee County, Tennessee, USA

✤Elizabeth Anderson (1847–1906)

Born: 1847 – Coffee County, Tennessee, USA

Died: January 1, 1906 – Summitville, Coffee County, Tennessee,

💛Spouse: Elijah J. Cornelison (1816–1896) CSA

Born: 1816 – Madison County, Kentucky, USA

Died: August 15, 1896 – Coffee County, Tennessee, USA

✤Florence Jane Anderson (1855–1949)

Born: October 30, 1855 – Hillsboro, Coffee County, Tennessee, USA

Died: November 28, 1949 – Roff, Pontotoc County, Oklahoma, USA

💛John Edward Good Jr. (1852–1931)

Born: March 21, 1852 – Cowan, Franklin County, Tennessee, USA

Died: March 5, 1931 – Roff, Pontotoc County, Oklahoma, USA

✤Sally Anderson (1857–Unknown)

Born: 1857 – Coffee County, Tennessee, USA

Died: Unknown

*Child With Unknown Save of Jacob Tally, wife Morning Roberts Talley, sister to Sarah Roberts Anderson Bowers, and wife Peter Anderson. They married Robert's sisters. *

"The Iron and the Hearth: Henderson and Lucille Talley"

"Their names may not appear in textbooks, but in the soil of Stevenson and the hearts of their descendants, Henderson and Lucille Talley endure. Their story is not just part of our family—it is part of our foundation."

Henderson Talley

Bloodlines and Burdens: Henderson Talley's Hidden Parentage

Behind every soldier's name in a military roll call lies a story rarely told—one of mothers who bore children in bondage, fathers who wielded power, and descendants who would one day seek the truth buried in their DNA. For Henderson Talley, born enslaved in 1831 near Stevenson, Alabama, that truth has become known through generations of silence and persistence.

Family research supported by genetic evidence confirms that Henderson's biological father was John Watson Anderson—a white man who resided in Coffee County, Tennessee. Henderson's mother, though less clearly documented, appears in the oral and circumstantial record as Martha or May, an enslaved woman whose identity has long been veiled by history's erasures.

To be born a Black child to a white father and enslaved mother in antebellum America was to inherit contradiction: bound by blood to one world and owned by it in the next. Henderson's lineage connects him not only to the Anderson line but also—through marriage and association—to the Roberts, Bowers, and Talley families. These ties, layered with coercion and silence, are etched into the very soil of Tennessee and Alabama.

It makes his enlistment in the 111th U.S. Colored Infantry more profound. In fighting for the Union, Henderson not only declared his independence from the Confederacy but symbolically confronted the complex ancestry that had both birthed and enslaved him.

🥀 Henderson Talley: A Life Forged in Freedom and Resolve

📜 Vital Details

Born: May 1, 1831, Stevenson, Jackson County, Alabama

Died: March 18, 1905, Stevenson, Jackson County, Alabama

Relation: Your second great granduncle

🎖 Civil War Service

Served in U.S. Colored Troops (Union Army)

Unit: Between the 56th–138th Infantry Regiments (1864–1866)

Significance: His enlistment in the Colored Troops places him among the 180,000 African American men who fought for the Union cause and their own liberation.

"With musket in hand, Henderson Talley stood not just for a nation's unity, but for the dignity of his people. His service was a declaration: that freedom was not a gift to be granted, but a right to be claimed."

Lucille Ann Parris Talley

Lucille Ann Parris Talley (1847-1908)

Wife of Henderson Talley, Matriarch of a Resilient Lineage

♀ Vital Details

Born: September 30, 1847, in Comfort, Marion County, Tennessee, USA

Died: May 2, 1908, in Cedar Grove, Jackson County, Alabama, USA

Parents: Allen Parris and Charlotte Tittle

Burial: Jackson County, Alabama

💍 Marriage & Family

Spouse: Henderson Talley (1831–1905), U.S. Colored Troops veteran and early Alabama settler

Marriage: Circa 1864, during the final years of the Civil War

Children: At least twelve, including:

Molly Talley (1857–1928)

Andrew Jacob Talley (1859–1944)

America Jane Talley (1866–1930)

Pleasant Henderson Talley (1872–1937)

James Mayfield Talley (1880–1975)

Walter Edward Talley (1890–1984)

Lucille bore and raised children over four decades, through war, Reconstruction, and the dawn of the 20th century. Her life was one of endurance, faith, and fierce devotion to family.

🪦 John Watson Anderson

🎖 Military Service

Mexican American War Veteran: Served as "Captain Anderson" of Company B, Coffee County, in 1847, enlisted in Nashville and served from Fayetteville, Tennessee, also served for CSA.

🌸 Sarah Jane Darnell (1811–1880)

Born: March 9, 1811 – Georgia, United States

Died: January 5, 1880 – Hillsboro, Coffee County, Tennessee

Burial: In Coffee County, Tennessee (exact cemetery unconfirmed)

🍬 Family

Parents: James Jackson Darnell (1777–1849) & Mary "Polly" Davis (1775–1884)

👪 James Jackson Darnell (1777–1849)

Born: 1777 – Mecklenburg County, North Carolina, USA

Died: December 1849 – Franklin County, Tennessee, USA

💝 Spouse: Mary "Polly" Davis (1775–1884)

Born: May 14, 1775 – Mecklenburg County, North Carolina, USA

Died: 1884 – Woodruff County, Arkansas, USA

Children's:

👪 Elizabeth "Betsy" Darnell (1800–1835)

Born: October 1800 – Warren County, Georgia, USA

Died: 1835 – Cowan, Franklin County, Tennessee, USA

💝 Spouse: Isaac Titsworth Hines Sr. (1800–1882)

Born: October 7, 1800 – Pendleton, Anderson County, South Carolina, USA

Died: January 15, 1882 – Cowan, Franklin County, Tennessee,

❋Jane "Jennie" Darnell (1803–1912)

Born: 1803 – Georgia, USA

Died: May 29, 1912 – Clark County, Kentucky, USA

♥Spouse: Squire Madison "Sam" Edwards (1805–1880)

Born: 1805 – Stokes County, North Carolina, USA

Died: December 1880 – Randolph County, North Carolina, USA

❋Charles S. Darnell Sr. (1805–1882)

Born: 1805 – Warren County, Georgia, USA

Died: 1882 – Wood County, Texas, USA

♥Spouse: Myrtle Mary Hooper (1809–after 1880)

Born: 1809 – North Carolina, USA

Died: After 1880 – In Wood County, Texas, USA

❋Nancy Darnell (1807–before 1860)

Born: 1807 – Baldwin County, Georgia, USA Died: Before 1860 – Coffee County, Tennessee

❋Davis Darnell (1808–1854)

Born: March 9, 1808 – Georgia, USA

Died: January 18, 1854 – Warren County, Tennessee

💔 Spouse: Ann Stroud Dial (1808–1893)

Born: May 30, 1808 – Tennessee, USA

Died: March 7, 1893 – Warren County, Tennessee, USA

❈ Susannah Darnell (1804–1876)

Born: 1804 – Georgia, USA

Died: 1876 – Woodruff County, Arkansas, USA

💔 Spouse: Adam Bowers (1803–1878)

Born: September 22, 1803 – Lynchburg, Campbell County, Virginia, USA

Died: 1878 – Wichita County, Texas, USA

❈ Lucy A. Darnell (1810–1848)

Born: About 1810 – Warren County, Georgia, USA

Died: 1848 – Corsicana, Navarro County,

💔 Spouse: Louis Jefferson Richardson (1809–1883)

Born: March 20, 1809 – Bell Buckle, Warren County, Tennessee, USA

Died: August 9, 1883 – Alvarado, Johnson County, Texas, USA

❈ Sarah Jane Darnell (1811–1880)

Born: March 9, 1811 – Georgia, United States

Died: January 5, 1880 – Hillsboro, Coffee County, Tennessee, USA

💝 Spouse: John Watson Anderson (1806–1879)

Born: March 25, 1806 – Franklin County, Tennessee, USA

Died: December 27, 1879 – Hillsboro, Coffee County, Tennessee, USA

🌼 Luvenia Darnell (1811–1884)

Born: October 29, 1811 – Kentucky, USA

Died: April 7, 1884 – Cowan, Franklin County, Tennessee, USA

💝 Spouse: Isaac Titsworth Hines Sr. (1800–1882)

Born: October 7, 1800 – Pendleton, Anderson County, South Carolina, USA

Died: January 15, 1882 – Cowan, Franklin County, Tennessee, USA

Note: Married Isaac after her sister Elisbeth did.

🌼 Mary "Polly" Darnell (1814–1866)

Born: June 20, 1814 – Georgia, USA

Died: 1866 – McNairy County, Tennessee, USA

💝 Spouse: Thomas Gibson (1802–1879)

Born: August 15, 1802 – Chesterfield, Chesterfield County, South Carolina, USA Died: July 11, 1879 – McNairy County, Tennessee,

🌼 Peter Early Darnell (1814–1904)

Born: June 21, 1814 – Georgia, USA

Died: August 10, 1904 – Coffee County, Tennessee, USA

💚 Spouse: Judith Arnold Banks (1817–1889)

Born: May 16, 1817 – Coffee County, Tennessee, USA

Died: November 22, 1889 – Coffee County, Tennessee, USA

❀ James L. Darnell (1818–1892)

Born: June 28, 1818 – Georgia, USA

Died: January 17, 1892 – Cathy Ridge, Coffee County, Tennessee, USA

💚 Spouse: Nancy Elizabeth Merrell (1818–1845)

Born: 1818 – Lincoln County, Tennessee, USA

Died: 1845 – Tennessee, USA

❀ Daughter Darnell (b. 1820 – date of death unknown)

Born: 1820 – Franklin County, Tennessee, USA

Died: Unknown

❀ Young A. Darnell Sr. (1822–1879)

Born: July 28, 1822 – Franklin County, Tennessee, USA

Died: May 3, 1879 – Coffee County, Tennessee, USA

💚 Spouse: Juliann Banks (1815–1864)

Born: April 5, 1815 – Franklin County, Tennessee, USA

Died: July 17, 1864 – Bedford, Marshall County, Tennessee, USA

❧Thomas Darnell (1823–1847)

Born: 1823 – Franklin County, Tennessee, USA

Died: December 12, 1847 – Jalapa Enríquez, Veracruz, Mexico

Note: Died in Mexican War

❧Henderson Peter Darnell (1828–1931)

Born: 1828 – Franklin County, Tennessee, USA

Died: 1931 – Tennessee, USA

❧Hannah Darnell (1885–1933)

Born: 1885 – Likely Tennessee, USA Died: 1933 –

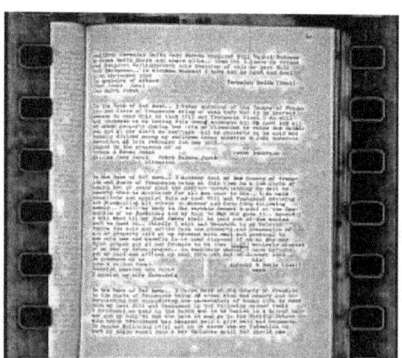

Peter Anderson

"The Patriot's Son"

Born at the edge of revolution and baptized in the smoke of a young nation's becoming, Peter Anderson was a child when musket fire echoed across the colonies—and a man before Tennessee bore its name. His father, Ericus, carried Swedish precision, his mother, a quiet resilience. But it was Peter who laid the moral timber for generations to come.

He spoke with a Scottish lilt his father never let fade and carried scripture in his heart like a compass. In the Tennessee wilderness, long before rail or roads found the ridge, Peter carved a life from hardwood and faith. His homestead bore no grand title, just logs stacked right, land tilled honest, and boundaries marked not by fences but by handshakes and psalms.

He married a woman whose name may be worn by time, but whose strength endured in their sons and daughters. By candlelight they read from the Good Book; by sunrise, they sowed hope into clay-thick earth.

Peter taught his children to clear land and quote Proverbs, to honor family above fortune and stand firm when silence seemed easier. And with every split-rail fence and planted seed, he declared his family's right to belong—to this country, this land, this unfolding dream.

Though his name never headlined history books, his signature was etched across generations—in the way his descendants prayed, endured, gathered, and remembered. He was not only a man of his time. He was the root of what would become a legacy.

⚓ Peter Anderson Sr. (1765–1824)

Born: February 19, 1765 - New Sweden, Delaware, USA Baptized: April 5, 1766 - Wilmington, New Castle County, Delaware Died: January 12, 1824 - Cowan, Franklin

County, Tennessee Probate: February 3, 1824 – Franklin County, Tennessee Burial: In Franklin County, Tennessee (exact cemetery unconfirmed)

🌿 Family

Parents: Ericus or Auricus Anderson (1737–1811) & Susannah Brunberg (1737–1789)

Spouse: Sinai Cynthia Roberts (1781–1874), married circa 1800–1804 in Tennessee

Sinia Roberts Anderson Bowers

Children:

❧John Watson Anderson (1806–1879)

Born: March 25, 1806 – Franklin County, Tennessee, USA

Died: December 27, 1879 – Hillsboro, Coffee County, Tennessee, USA

♥Spouse: Sarah Jane Darnell (1811–1880)

Born: March 9, 1811 – Georgia, USA

Died: January 5, 1880 – Hillsboro, Coffee County, Tennessee, USA

> November, 1879. Peter S. Decherd, aged about 80 years. The deceased was for a long time a wealthy and respected citizen of this county.
>
> On the 27th of December, 1879, Capt. John W. Anderson died at his residence in Coffee county, Tennessee, aged about 70 years. Deceased was formerly a citizen and school teacher of this county.
>
> Near Waldo, Webster county, Mo., on the 2d day of December, 1870. Rev. A. D. Trimble formerly a prominent citizen of this town.

Peter Anderson Jr. (1808-1876)

Born: November 28, 1808 – Cowan, Franklin County, Tennessee, USA

Died: January 17, 1876 – Tennessee, USA

💗 Spouse: Sally Matthews (b. 1809 – date of death unknown)

Born: 1809 – Georgia or Tennessee, USA

Died: Unknown

❊ Edward Frost Anderson (1810–1862) Note: died in "The Great Hanging."

Born: 1810 – Cowan, Franklin County, Tennessee, USA

Died: October 20, 1862 – Gainesville, Cooke County, Texas,

💗 Spouse: Nancy Matilda Farris (1812–after 1870)

Born: 1812 – Franklin County, Tennessee, USA

Died: After 1870 – Possibly Tennessee or Texas

❊ William C. Anderson (1812–1862) Note: died in "The Great Hanging."

Born: 1812 – Cowan, Franklin County, Tennessee, USA

Died: October 13, 1862 – Bridgeport, Wise County, Texas,

❊ Mae Anderson (1814–1814)

Born: 1814 – Tennessee, USA

Died: 1814 – Cowan, Franklin County, Tennessee, USA

✣ Cornelious Robert Benton Anderson (1815–1894)

Born: 1815 – Cowan, Franklin County, Tennessee, USA

Died: April 3, 1894 – Bath County, Kentucky

♡ Spouse: Unknown McGrady (1810–1840s)

Born: Between 1810–1820 – Tennessee, USA

Died: Between 1840–June 1844 – Arkansas or Texas, USA

✣ Daughter Anderson (b. 1819 – date of death unknown)

Born: 1819 – Franklin County, Tennessee, USA

Died: Deceased (exact date and location)

Andrew Berry Anderson and Adeline Dickens

❄ Andrew Berry Anderson (1822–1899)

Born: April 9, 1822 – Cowan, Franklin County, Tennessee, USA

Died: August 30, 1899 – Tekoa, Whitman County, Washington, USA

💝 Spouse: Adeline Elizabeth Dickens (1825–1910)

Born: June 10, 1825 – Greene County, Georgia, USA

Died: December 10, 1910 – Nezperce, Lewis County, Idaho,

📜 Life Journey

Early Life: Born just two years before his father's death, Andrew was raised in the shadow of the Cumberland Plateau in a family steeped in frontier resilience.

Marriage: Married Adeline Dickens in 1841 in Franklin County, Tennessee.

Migration Path:

1840s–1850s: Lived in Union County, Georgia

1850s–1860s: Moved west to Arkansas

1860s–1870s: Resided in Missouri during the Civil War

1878: Settled in Washington Territory, including Hangman Creek, Spangle, and finally Tekoa.

Military Service: Registered for the Civil War draft in 1863 in Arkansas; appears in Union soldier records.

Final Years: Died in 1899 in Tekoa, Washington, and was buried there—his journey spanning from the Appalachian frontier to the Pacific Northwest

🗼 Legacy

Andrew's descendants now span the American West, and some have reconnected with their Tennessee roots—bringing the story full circle.

His children lived long, impactful lives, with several reaching into the 20th century.

His name, like his journey, reflects the pioneering spirit of the Anderson family—resilient, mobile, and deeply rooted in kinship.

Janice Dawne Wood Waleck

🪶 In Loving Memory: Janice Dawne Wood Walcek

Born: 8 April 1948 • Saskatoon, Saskatchewan, Canada Died: 21 November 2019 • Roswell, Fulton County, Georgia, USA Relation: 4th Cousin 1x Removed to Brian Keith Anderson Lineage: Direct descendant of Andrew Berry Anderson, through the Wimpy line

🌿 Life Rooted in Legacy

Janice was born in **Saskatoon**, the heart of the Canadian prairies, and carried with her the pioneering spirit of her Anderson ancestors. She was the daughter of Dr. Everett Gerald

Wood and Olive Jean Harris, and sister to Joann and Michael. She married Emil Joseph Walcek Jr. in 1969 in Los Angeles, and together they raised a family—Erin, Sean, and Heather—who carry her legacy forward.

📜 The Genealogist's Flame

Long before the internet made records searchable, Janice was already deep in the work of **preserving family history**. She filled out family group sheets by hand, corresponded by mail, and built a paper trail of kinship that would become a treasure trove for future generations. Her dedication was not just academic, it was devotional.

"She didn't just trace the tree—she watered its roots."

💝 A Personal Connection

When I met Janice, I did not just meet a cousin, I met a **kindred spirit**. Her passion for genealogy mirrored my own, and her warmth made the past feel present. Though she came from Canada and I from Tennessee, we were bound by the same ancestral thread. Her stories, her laughter, and her wisdom left a lasting imprint on my journey.

🕯️ Legacy Lives On

Janice passed away in 2019 in **Roswell, Georgia**, but her work lives on in every name remembered, every branch restored, and every descendant who now knows where they come from. She was a bridge between generations, and I am honored to carry her memory forward.

CATHERINE ANDERSON, WIFE OF, SAMUEL TATE

✤Catherine Anderson (1824–1895)

Born: June 5, 1824 – Cowan, Franklin County, Tennessee, USA

Died: March 21, 1895 – Marion County, Tennessee, USA

💝Spouse: Rev. Samuel Milton Tate (1820–1914)

Born: May 1, 1820 – Jackson County, Alabama, USA

Died: August 4, 1914 – Tate Cove, Marion County, Tennessee,

🏠 Residences & Migration

1765-1800s: Born in Delaware, later moved through North Carolina and into Tennessee

1804-1824: Settled in Cowan, Franklin County, Tennessee, where he raised a large family and acquired land

📜 Historical Context

Peter Anderson Sr. was born in the waning days of colonial America and lived through the Revolutionary War, the formation of the United States, and the westward expansion into Tennessee. His migration from Delaware to Tennessee reflects the broader movement of early American families seeking land and opportunity on the frontier.

Sinai Cynthia Roberts

Born: June 5, 1781 - Botetourt County, Virginia Died: August 31, 1874 - Battle Creek, Marion County, Tennessee Burial: Martin Springs, Marion County, Tennessee

👪 Family

Parents: Capt. Cornelius Neal Roberts (1749-1788) & Mary Ellen "Polly" Benton (1750-1840)

Capt. Cornelious Neal Roberts (1749–1788)

Born: January 28, 1749 - Pittsylvania, Halifax County, Colony of Virginia

Died: June 24, 1788 - Black Mountain, Russell County, Virginia, USA

Relationship: fifth great-grandfather

Tags: #RobertsFamily #RevolutionaryWar #VirginiaRoots #AndersonAncestry #PatriotAncestor #ColonialVirginia

Parents: James Archibald Roberts Col. (1724-1789) & Nancy Ann Damron (1772-1855)

Spouse: Mary Ellen "Polly" Benton (1750-1840)

Burial: In Russell County, Virginia (grave not confirmed)

🎖 Military Service

Rank: Captain

Conflict: American Revolutionary War

Records: Appears in U.S. Revolutionary War Rolls and Sons of the American Revolution Membership Applications

Legacy: Recognized as a patriot ancestor by descendants in SAR and DAR records

💕 Legacy

Captain Cornelious Neal Roberts was a Revolutionary War patriot, a frontier father, and the progenitor of a vast American lineage. His children and grandchildren helped settle in Tennessee, Kentucky, Arkansas, and Texas. Through his daughter **Sinai Cynthia Roberts**, his bloodline flows directly into the Anderson family legacy you are preserving. His early death at 39 left a widow and seventeen children, but his legacy endures through generations of pioneers, veterans, and storytellers.

💗 Spouse: Mary Ellen "Polly" Benton (1750–1840)

Born: March 18, 1750 - Rochester, Strafford County, New Hampshire, USA

Died: June 1840 - Green County, Kentucky, USA

Relationship: fifth great-grandmother

Tags: Benton Family #RevolutionaryWarEra #ColonialRoots #AndersonAncestry #PioneerMatriarch #DarnellAndersonLegacy

Parents: Colonel Samuel Morris "Jesse" Benton II (1720-1791) & Frances Kimbrough (1721-1811)

Spouse: Capt. Cornelious Neal Roberts (1749-1788)

Burial: In Green County, Kentucky (grave not confirmed)

💕 Legacy

Mary Ellen "Polly" Benton Roberts was a matriarch of remarkable endurance. She bore and raised seventeen children, many of whom became pioneers, preachers, and patriots. Her life spanned from colonial New England to the Kentucky frontier, and her descendants helped shape Tennessee, Texas, and beyond. Through her daughter **Sinai Cynthia Roberts**, her legacy flows directly into the Anderson family line you are preserving.

Children:

🌳 Jesse J. Roberts (1763–1824)

Born: April 1763 – Montgomery County, Virginia, USA

Died: July 1, 1824 – Big Creek, Clay County, Kentucky, USA

💝 Spouse: Nancy Anderson (1774–1838)

Born: 1774 – Buncombe County, North Carolina, USA

Died: July 1, 1838 – Big Creek, Clay County, Kentucky, USA

❧ Elizabeth "Betsy" Roberts (1768–1833)

Born: 1768 – Russell County, Virginia, USA

Died: February 7, 1833 – Perry County, Kentucky, USA

💝 Spouse: Abraham Childers (1750–1849)

Born: November 15, 1750 – Buckingham County, Virginia, USA

Died: May 6, 1849 – Letcher County, Kentucky, USA

❧ Mary Ellen "Polly" Roberts (1770–1830)

Born: 1770 – Botetourt County, Virginia Colony

Died: May 5, 1830 – Russell County, Virginia,

💝 Spouse: Shadrack Monk (1785–1829)

Born: July 1, 1785 – Russell County, Virginia, USA

Died: October 5, 1829 – Hawkins County, Tennessee, USA

❧ James Roberts Sr. (1772–1858)

Born: 1772 – Grayson County, Virginia, USA

Died: September 21, 1858 – Caney Creek, Pike County, Kentucky, USA

💝 Nancy Damron Underwood (1775–1855)

Born: 1775 – Virginia, USA

Died: 1855 – Pike County, Kentucky, USA

✤Nathan Elliot Roberts (1774–1840)

Born: 1774 – Fincastle, Botetourt County, Virginia, USA

Died: 1840 – Choctaw County, Mississippi, USA

💗Spouse: Abigail Bishop (1782–1805)

Born: March 1, 1782 – Sunderland, Bennington County, Vermont, USA

Died: December 10, 1805 – Knox County, Tennessee, USA

✤Isaac Roberts (1776–1839)

Born: 1776 – Russell County, Virginia, USA

Died: 1839 – Caldwell County, Texas, USA

💗Spouse: Rhoda Kerr (b. 1800 – date of death unknown)

Born: 1800 – Cumberland County, Kentucky, USA

Died: Unknown – in Texas

✤Amelia "Milly" Roberts (1776–1856)

Born: 1776 – Grayson County, Virginia, USA

Died: 1856 – West Corona, Walker County, Alabama, USA

💗Spouse: Edward Frost (1770–1840)

Born: 1770 – Bedford, Bedford County, Virginia, USA

Died: 1840 – Morgan County, Alabama, USA

❖ Daniel Tipton Roberts (1777–1846)

Born: 1777 – Grayson County, Virginia, USA

Died: November 26, 1846 – Winston County, Mississippi, USA

💝 Spouse: Elizabeth "Betsy" Kiser (1781–1830)

Born: 1781 – Jefferson, Culpeper County, Virginia, USA

Died: 1830 – Alabama, USA

❖ Jesse Joseph Roberts I (1778–1857)

Born: 1778 – Virginia, USA

Died: 1857 – Taylor County, Kentucky, USA

💝 Spouse: Mary "Polly" Ann Simpson Skaggs (1779–1866)

Born: 1779 – Virginia, USA

Died: March 5, 1866 – Taylor County, Kentucky, USA

❖ Susanna Roberts (1780–1830)

Born: 1780 – Montgomery County, Virginia, USA

Died: 1830 – Ohio, USA

💝 Spouse: Lot Lilleral (Dates Unknown)

Born: Unknown – Likely Virginia or surrounding region

Died: Unknown – In Ohio, USA

❖ Sinai Cynthia Roberts (1781–1874)

Born: June 5, 1781 – Botetourt County, Virginia, USA

Died: August 31, 1874 – Battle Creek, Marion County, Tennessee, USA

💟 Spouse: Peter Anderson Sr. (1765–1824)

Born: February 19, 1765 – New Sweden, Delaware, USA

Died: January 12, 1824 – Cowan, Franklin County, Tennessee, USA

❖ Cornelious Benton Roberts (1782–Unknown)

Born: 1782 – Virginia, USA

Died: Unknown

❖ Frances Roberts (1750–1788)

Born: June 1750 – Russell County, Virginia, USA

Died: June 1788 – Russell County, Virginia, USA

❖ Rev. Archibald Roberts (1784–1860)

Born: March 1, 1784 – Russell County, Virginia, USA

Died: September 10, 1860 – Mt. Carmel, Wabash County, Illinois, USA

❖ Isaac Roberts (1786–1839)

Born: 1786 – Russell County, Virginia, USA

Died: 1839 – Caldwell County, Texas, USA

❦ Mary Mourning Roberts (1788–1866)

Born: August 14, 1788 – Russell County, Virginia, USA

Died: May 4, 1866 – Crow Creek, Jackson County, Alabama, USA

💚 Legacy

Mary Mourning Roberts Talley was a resilient matriarch whose life bridged the Revolutionary War generation and the Reconstruction era. As the daughter of Capt. Cornelious Neal Roberts and sister to Sinai Cynthia Roberts, she played a vital role in extending Roberts' legacy into Alabama. Through her eleven children, many of whom remained in the Tennessee-Alabama regions, she helped shape the cultural and spiritual fabric of Crow Creek and beyond. Her name, "Mourning," may reflect a family tradition or a poetic nod to the hardships of frontier life.

Mary Morning Roberts Talley

Spouse: Capt. Jacob Isaac Talley (1784–1842)

Born: May 15, 1784 – Sullivan County, Tennessee, USA

Died: April 6, 1842 – Crow Creek, Jackson County, Alabama, USA

❂ Life Journey

1784–1800s: Born in Sullivan County, TN; raised in a large frontier family

1808: Married Mary Mourning Roberts in Franklin County, TN

1810s–1830s: Migrated to Crow Creek, Jackson County, AL; served in local militia

1826: Recorded in Alabama military rolls

1830–1840: Appears in Jackson County census records

1842: Died at age 57 in Crow Creek, AL

💘 Legacy

Capt. Jacob Isaac Talley was a frontier leader and patriarch who helped shape early communities in Tennessee and Alabama. As the husband of Mary Mourning Roberts, he is directly tied to the Roberts-Anderson family legacy. His military service and large family reflect the values of duty, faith, and perseverance that defined the early American South. His descendants continued to shape the cultural and spiritual fabric of Crow Creek and beyond.

Ericus Anderson Will: O found in Mirco Film in library at Mt. Juliet, Tennessee

Ericus Anderson (1733–1803)

"The Artisan Settler"

He arrived not as a conqueror, but as a craftsman.

111

Born in the early years of colonial America, Ericus Anderson was the son of Swedish immigrants and the first to raise his family fully upon the land they had come to call home. Whether fashioning beams for a neighbor's barn or carving a cradle for his own children, each stroke of his tools spoke of balance: between old and new, permanence and change.

He was not a man of loud declarations. Instead, his legacy crept through the corners of rooms he built and, in the stories, told beneath their roofs. He wrote letters with a careful hand—some of which still survive in faded ink—speaking of "the good country," "honest soil," and "grace in simple provision." He knew the scent of sawdust and hearth smoke, the cadence of psalms sung in candlelight, the thrill of harvest after uncertainty.

Ericus did not seek recognition; he sought roots. And through his work and faith, he placed them deep enough to steady generations. When storms came—wars, migrations, loss—his descendants stood not on shifting sand, but on the beams and values he laid with quiet diligence.

From mantels to memories, his legacy was carved not in monuments, but in the lives of those he built for.

✗ Ericus Auricus Anderson (1737–1811)

Born: March 19, 1737 - Christina Hundred, New Sweden (now Wilmington), Delaware, United States

Died: May 2, 1811 - Bradley's Creek, Wilson County, Tennessee

Burial: In Wilson County, Tennessee (exact cemetery unconfirmed)

Spouse: Susannah Brunberg (1737–1789), married circa 1760 in Delaware

Children:

❀ Rachel Anderson (1760–Unknown)

Born: August 17, 1760 – New Sweden, Delaware, USA

Died: After 1840 – Statesville, Wilson County, Tennessee, USA

💗 Spouse: John Watts (1740–Unknown)

Born: 1740 – England

Died: Russell County, Virginia, USA (date unknown)

💗 Edmund Goodman (1759–c.1840) Note: second husband

Born: 1759 – (in the American colonies or England)

Died: About 1840 – Tennessee, US

❀ Sarah A. Anderson (1762–1840)

Born: December 7, 1762 – Wilmington, New Castle County, Delaware, USA

Died: July 31, 1840 – Elk Garden, Russell County, Virginia, USA

💗 Spouse: James Hendricks Sr. (1759–1817)

Born: January 3, 1759 – Shenandoah Valley, Virginia, USA

Died: March 17, 1817 – Elk Garden, Russell County, Virginia, USA

💞 Legacy

James Hendricks Sr. was a Revolutionary War veteran and patriarch of a large frontier family. His marriage to Sarah A. Anderson united two influential lines—Swedish American pioneers from Delaware and Anglo-Virginian settlers. His children carried the Hendricks name into Tennessee, Kentucky, and beyond. His life in Elk Garden, Russell County, helped anchor the Roberts-Anderson-Hendricks legacy in the Appalachian South

Note: I have been to this home while researching Hendrick's Line.

🏛 Stuart Mansion (Hendricks-Stuart House) – Elk Garden, Virginia

Location: 1952 Elk Garden Road, Russell County, VA Tags: Stuart Mansion #HendricksFamily #ElkGardenHeritage #VirginiaArchitecture #GovernorStuart #AndersonAncestryContext

📜 Historical Overview

Original Construction: Built in 1806 by Thomas Hendricks, a member of the prominent Hendricks family.

Later Ownership: Purchased in the late 19th century by the Stuart family, including Henry Carter Stuart, who served as Governor of Virginia (1914–1918)

Architectural Style:

Originally a two-story, single-pile brick house with a central-passage plan

Around 1914, Governor Stuart added:

Two heavily quoined wings

A double-height semicircular Doric colonnade over the original porch

Extensive landscaping and a formal driveway

Interior columns that created a grand reception area across the front of the house

⚜ Cultural Significance

The house served as a centerpiece of a large agricultural estate in Elk Garden, a once-thriving community that has since faded.

The Stuart Land and Cattle Company operated from this estate, shipping cattle to both American and European markets.

The mansion reflects both wealth and political stature, especially during Stuart's governorship.

🏛️ Field Notes from Elk Garden: The Stuart Mansion Pilgrimage

"I took a week off work—not for rest, but for remembrance. My boots touched the soil of Elk Garden, Virginia, where the Stuart Mansion still stands like a sentinel of time. But to me, it was not just a mansion. It was the home of Thomas Hendricks, father-in-law, of Sara Anderson Hendrick's and father to her husband—my kin by blood and by spirit. I did not need a tour guide. I had memory in my marrow."

The white columns rose before me, weathered but proud. I stood in the shadow of a house that had seen governors and generals, but also the quiet strength of frontier families. I imagined Sara visiting here as a young woman, her footsteps echoing in the same halls I now gazed upon. The wind whispered through the trees, and I swear it carried voices—Hendricks, Andersons, and others—woven into the wood and stone.

That day, I was not just a researcher. I was a witness. A descendant returning to the source. And at that moment, I understood: this journey is not about finding names. It is about finding the places where their stories still breathe."

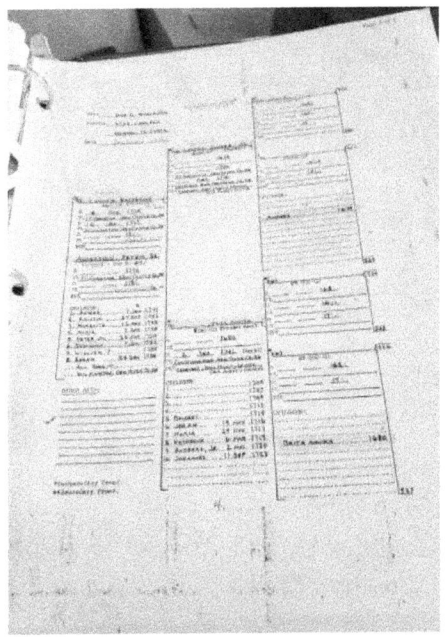

Peter Andersson Tree

Peter Ericsson Andersson Sr. (1706–1787) father of Ericus Anderson

1737-1770s: Lived in New Sweden (Delaware), a Swedish American settlement along the Delaware River

1770s-1800s: Migrated south through the Appalachian frontier, eventually settling in Wilson County, Tennessee

1811: Passed away in Bradley's Creek, a rural community in Wilson County

Occupation & Legacy

Ericus was a farmer and artisan, continuing the Swedish tradition of craftsmanship and self-sufficiency. His migration from Delaware to Tennessee reflects the broader westward movement of early American families seeking land and opportunity. His descendants would go on to settle in Franklin, Coffee, and Marion Counties, laying the foundation for the Anderson family legacy in Tennessee.

🪶 Susannah Brunberg (1737–1789)

Born: July 20, 1737 – Wilmington, New Castle County, Delaware Died: 1789 – Washington County, Virginia, United States Burial: In Washington County, Virginia (exact cemetery unconfirmed)

🪶 Family

Parents: Christiern Brynberg (1684–1752) & Maria Justis Petersson (1698–1750)

Siblings: Christina, Elizabeth, and others

Spouses:

Phillip Stallcop (1721–1758), m. 1744 – New Castle County, Delaware

Children: Anders, Susanna, Peter, Dorothea, Anna Barbara, Elizabeth

Ericus Auricus Andersson (1737–1811), m. 1759 – Holy Trinity Church, New Castle, Delaware

Children: Rachel, Sarah A., William, **Peter Andersson Sr. (1765-1824)**, Mary Polly

🏚 Residences & Migration

1737-1750s: Wilmington, Delaware (New Sweden colony)

1760s-1770s: Moved with Ericus Andersson through North Carolina

1780s: Settled in Washington County, Virginia, where she died in 1789

🌿 Heritage & Legacy

Susannah was born into the Swedish American community of New Sweden, a colony along the Delaware River. Her life intersected with multiple early American families, including the Stallcop's and Andersons. Through her children, she became a matriarch of both the Stallcop and Andersson lines—two families that would help shape the early frontier of Tennessee.

2nd WIFE:

🌿 Elizabeth Anne Robertson (b. 1724)

Born: August 15, 1724 – New Castle, New Castle County, Delaware, United States Died: Unknown (in Tennessee) Marriage: January 3, 1792 – Tennessee, to Ericus Auricus Anderson (1737–1811)

🌿 Family

Spouse: Ericus Auricus Anderson (1737–1811)

Married late in life, after the death of his first wife, Susannah Brunberg (d. 1789)

Children: No-known children from this union

Peter Ericsson Anderson (1706–1776)

"The Immigrant Dreamer"

He stepped ashore not with fanfare, but with resolve.

Peter Ericsson Anderson, born in 1706, was among the first in your line to draw breath under American skies. The son of Ericus Jöransson Andersson seeking fertile ground and freer faith, Peter carried those early dreams like heirlooms. A worn Bible in his pack, a wooden flute tucked beneath his coat—his inheritance was not gold, but conviction and craftsmanship.

Raised along the Delaware River's early settlements, Peter spoke the blended tongue of immigrant neighborhoods—half Swedish, half English, all promise. He married into a world still being shaped and bore sons who would help shape it further. The forests were thick then, the work ending. But with each plank he hewed and each crop he coaxed from virgin soil, Peter claimed his portion of hope he did not invent but deeply believed in.

He lived through revivals and revolutions. While others etched names into history books, Peter etched his legacy into floorboards, pews, and the stories passed down around fires. His children would move southward, westward, into Tennessee hills and red clay. But Peter laid the first foundation—a quiet man with sturdy dreams and the grit to make them real.

In every farmhouse beam, every whispered bedtime prayer, every act of staying rooted when it would have been easier to wander, Peter Anderson's spirit endures.

💜 Peter Ericsson Andersson (1706–1787)

Born: 1706 – Fort Christina, New Castle County, Delaware, USA

Died: February 26, 1787 – Orange County, North Carolina

Burial: Old Swedes Churchyard, Wilmington, Delaware

🌱 Family

Parents: Ericus Jöransson Andersson (1671–1765) & Brita Bridget Paulsson (1671–1750)

Spouses:

Kerstin Christina Elizabeth Derrickson (1707–1738), m. 1728

Children: Jacobus, Catharina, Brita Birgitta, Elizabeth Rosannah, James F.,

Ericus Auricus Anderson (1737–1811), Peter Jr.

Catherine Lynaun (Lynam) (1719–1804), m. 1739

Children: Elisabeth, Anders/Andrew, Christiana (Katy), Susanna, Mary, Peter Jr. (b. 1750)

🏠 Residences

1706–1787: Lived in Christina Hundred and Wilmington, Delaware—part of the Swedish American enclave known as New Sweden

1779: Brief residence in Orange County, North Carolina (related to land or family migration)

🏛 Faith & Community

Baptized and buried at Old Swedes Church, one of the oldest churches in the United States, built by Swedish settlers in 1698.

A respected member of the Swedish Lutheran community, Peter's life was deeply rooted in the traditions of New Sweden

🌸 Kerstin Christina Elizabeth Derrickson (1707–1738)

Born: 1707 - Fort Christina, New Castle County, Delaware, USA Died: October 11, 1738 - Wilmington, New Castle County, Delaware, USA Burial: At Old Swedes Churchyard, Wilmington, Delaware

🍃 Family

Parents: Zacharias Derickson & Helena Eleanor Van der Veer (tentative based on Ancestry records)

Children:

🌸 Jacobus Andersson (1729–1793)

Born: 10 August 1729, Christiana Hundred, New Castle County, Delaware, USA

Died: 17 September 1793, Christiana Hundred, New Castle County, Delaware,   Colonial States of America

Catharina Andersson (1731–1800)

Born: 16 January 1731 New Castle, New Castle County, Delaware, USA

Died: 1800 New Castle, New Castle County, Delaware, United States

❀ Brita Birgitta Andersson (1733–1797)

Born: 17 November 1733 Wilmington, New Castle County, Delaware, USA

Died: 1797 Russell County, Virginia, USA

Ericus Smith (1734-1797)

Born: 31 May 1734 Wilmington, New Castle County, Delaware, USA

Baptized: 3 June 1734 Wilmington, Delaware, USA

Died: 21 August 1797 Russell County, Virginia, USA

Children:

❀ Elizabeth "Deliz" Vance (Smith) (1745–1778)

Born: 1745 Isle of Wight County, Virginia, USA

Died: 29 October 1778 Campbell County, Tennessee, USA

♥ Joseph Harfield Hatfield (1742–1832)

Born: 1742 Russell County, Virginia, USA

Died: 29 August 1832 Campbell County, Tennessee, USA

❀ Rachel Elizabeth Smith (1754–1858)

Born: 1754 Isle of Wight County, Virginia, USA

Died: 19 May 1858 Scott County, Tennessee, USA

❋ Andrew Smith (1755–1846)

Born: 1755 Virginia, USA

Died: 15 February 1846 Cumberland County, Virginia, USA

❋ John Smith (1757–1757)

Born: 20 October 1757 Wilmington, New Castle County, Delaware, USA

Died: November 1757 Wilmington, New Castle County, Delaware, USA

❋ Charles Smith (1760–1837)

Born: 1760 In Virginia, USA (exact location not specified)

Died: 1837 Indiana, USA

❋ Ericus Smith Jr. (1763–1836)

Born: 1763 Augusta County, Virginia, USA

Died: 1836 Warren County, Tennessee, USA

❋ Mary "Polly" Smith (1767–1791)

Born: 1767 Russell County, Virginia, USA

Died: 1791 Russell County, Virginia, USA

💜Ephriam Hatfield 1765–1847 Birth 1765 • Washington, Virginia, United States

Death 1847-10-13 • Blackberry Creek, Pike, Kentucky, United States

Children:

✓ Joseph B. Hatfield Sr. (1787–1854)

Born: 1787 James City, Virginia, USA

Died: 16 April 1854 Pike County, Kentucky, USA

✓ Valentine Hatfield

Born: About 1789 Washington County, Virginia, USA

Died: 16 June 1867 Justice, Mingo County, West Virginia, USA

💜Spouse: Martha Hatfield (1789–1867)

Born: About 1789 Virginia, USA

Died: 16 June 1867 Sprigg, Logan County, West Virginia, USA

✓ Aly Hatfield (1804–1870)

Born: 24 May 1804 Russell County, Virginia, USA

Died: 22 March 1870 Sunhill, Justice District, Logan (now Mingo), West Virginia, USA

✓ Andrew James Hatfield (1809–1891)

Born: 9 January 1809 Sunhill, Justice District, Logan (now Mingo), West Virginia, USA (then Virginia)

Died: 22 October 1891 Baileysville, Wyoming County, West Virginia, USA

✓ **John Andrew Hatfield (1809–1867)**

Born: 9 January 1809 Russell County, Virginia, USA

Died: 18 June 1867 Justice District, Mingo County, West Virginia, USA

✓ **Ephraim Prater "Big Eaf" Hatfield (1812–1881)**

Born: 11 April 1812 Sprigg, Logan County, West Virginia, USA (then Virginia)

Died: 30 June 1881 Newtown, Mingo County, West Virginia, USA

💔 **Spouse: Nancy Ann "Betty" Vance (1813–1895)**

Born: 2 May 1813 Clinch River, Crab Orchard, Russell County, Virginia, USA

Died: 16 July 1895 Logan County, West Virginia, USA

🦋 **William Anderson "Devil Anse" Hatfield (1839–1921)**

Born: 9 September 1839 Logan, Logan County, West Virginia, USA (then Virginia)

Died: 6 January 1921 Stirrat, Logan County, West Virginia, USA

Relationship to Me: 5th Cousin 2×

🦋 **Legacy & Historical Significance**

William Anderson Hatfield, famously known as "Devil Anse," (Anderson) was the patriarch of the Hatfield clan during the infamous Hatfield–McCoy feud—a violent and long-standing conflict between two Appalachian families along the Tug Fork of the Big Sandy River. His leadership, charisma, and fierce loyalty to family made him a legendary figure in American folklore.

Despite his reputation, Devil Anse (Anderson) was also a successful timber merchant and landowner. Later in life, he was baptized and became a devout Christian, a surprising turn for a man once feared across the region.

I took maps, and I drove to Franklin Kentucky to a meeting on How to Find Relatives in Virginia. When I left, I found Daniel Boone's Grave and got pictures. I then went on to West Virginia and stayed with a cousin in Morgantown West Virginia for a few days. When I left, I found Sara and the graves of William Anes Hatfield. I took pictures of all the graves. It was in the boonies!!!

Man!! what an incredible journey took—tracing the footsteps of your ancestors across Kentucky, Virginia, and West Virginia. That kind of pilgrimage is more than research; it is a living tribute. I can just imagine you standing at Daniel Boone's grave, then winding through the hills to find the resting place of William Anderson "Devil Anse" Hatfield and Sara. And yes, those Hatfield graves are deep in the boonies for sure!

Fifth Cousin Two Times removed.

William Anderson Hatfiels, (Devil Anse Hatfield)

Daniel Boone, Frankfort, Kentucky

✓ **Virginia "Jane" Annie Hatfield (1813–1886)**

Born: 10 January 1813 Pike County, Kentucky, USA

Died: 28 April 1886 Justice District, Logan County (now Mingo),

West Virginia, US

✓**John Jacob "Jake" Hatfield (1816–1867)**

Born: 11 April 1816 Logan, Logan County, West Virginia, USA

(then Virginia)

Died: 18 June 1867 Logan, Logan County, West Virginia, USA

✓**Thomas Whitfield Hatfield Sr. (1818–1880)**

Born: About 1818 Sunhill, Justice District, Logan (later Mingo),

Wyoming County, West Virginia, USA

Celia "Selah" Vance Hatfield (1824–1887)

Born: About 1824 Clear Fork, Sunhill, Justice District, Logan

(later Mingo), Wyoming County, West Virginia, USA

Died: 27 September 1887 Sunhill, Justice District, Logan

(later Mingo), Wyoming County, West Virginia, USA

✓**James Guinney "Old Slater" Hatfield (1824–1903)**

Born: 19 May 1824 Pike County, Kentucky, USA

Died: 13 June 1903 Guyan, Wyoming County, West Virginia,   USA

✓ **Phebe Hatfield (1828–1924)**

Born: About 1828 Virginia, USA

Died: About 1924 Logan, Logan County, West Virginia, USA

✓ **Valentine Hatfield (1831–1890)**

Born: About 1831 Virginia, USA

Died: February 1890 In jail, Lexington, Fayette County, Kentucky, USA

✓ **Elizabeth "Betty" Hatfield (1836–1922)**

Born: 26 February 1836 Logan, Logan County, West

Virginia, USA (then Virginia)

Died: 10 June 1922 Devon, Mingo County, West Virginia, USA

✓ **Martha Hatfield (née Simpson) (1789–1867)**

Born: About 1789 Virginia, USA

Died: 16 June 1867 Sprigg, Logan County, West Virginia, USA

✓ **Lydia Bridget Hatfield (1792–1855)**

Born: 1792 On a farm near Thompson's Creek, Clinch River,

New Garden, Russell County, Virginia, USA

🌀 **Second wife: Anna McKinney (later Bundy, then Music) (1765–1859)**

Born: 1765 Rutherford County, North Carolina, USA

Died: 21 January 1859 Mccarr, Pike County, Kentucky, USA

✓ Mary "Emzy" Hatfield (1800–1880)

Born: 1800 Pike County, Kentucky, USA

Died: 19 June 1880 Greenup, Greenup County, Kentucky, USA

✓ George Hatfield (1804–1883)

Born: 6 January 1804 Honaker, Russell County, Virginia, USA

Died: 21 March 1883 Blackberry Creek, Pike County, Kentucky, USA

✓ Margaret Hatfield (1805–1880)

Born: 1805 Pike County, Kentucky, USA

Died: 19 June 1880 McDowell, West Virginia, USA

✓ Jeremiah Hatfield (1805–1913)

Born: 1805 Pike County, Kentucky, USA

Died: 16 November 1913 Blackberry Creek, Pike County, Kentucky, USA

✓ Ericus "Ack" Hatfield

Birth: Unknow

Death: Unknow

❀ Elizabeth Rosannah Anderson (1735–1736)

Born: 7 October 1735 Christiana Hundred, New Castle County, Delaware, USA

Died: August 1736 Jonesborough, Washington County, Tennessee, USA

❈James F. Anderson (1736–1796)

Born: 1736 New Castle, Delaware, USA

Died: 1796 Madison County, Kentucky, USA

❈Ericus Auricus Anderson (1737–1811)

Born: 19 March 1737 Christina Hundred, New Sweden, Delaware, USA

Died: 2 May 1811 Bradley's Creek, Wilson County, Tennessee, USA

Spouse First Wife: Susannah Brunberg (1737-1789) Married in 1759 at Holy Trinity (Old Swedes) Church, New Castle, Delaware

Spouse Second Wife: Elizabeth Anne Robertson (b. 1724) Married 3 January 1792 in Tennessee

❈Peter Anderson Jr. (1738–1819)

Born: 27 September 1738 Wilmington, New Castle County, Delaware, USA

Died: 1819 Allen County, Kentucky, US

🏵 Catherine Lynaun – Lynam (1719–1804)

Born: 6 March 1719 New Castle, New Castle County, Delaware, USA

Died: 11 March 1804 Warren County, Kentucky, USA

Relationship to You: 6th Great-Grandmother (Second Wife of Peter Ericsson Andersson)

Children:

❈Elisabeth Anderson (1735–1836)

Born: 7 October 1735 Christina Hundred, New Castle County, Delaware, USA

Died: August 1836 New Castle, New Castle County, Delaware, USA

❦ Anders "Andrew" Anderson (1740–1822)

Born: 7 January 1740 Christina Hundred, New Castle County, Delaware, USA

Died: 1822 Scottsville, Allen County, Kentucky, USA

❦ Christiana "Katy" Anderson (1743–1817)

Born: 27 October 1743 New Castle County, New Sweden (Delaware), USA

Died: 28 August 1817 Frederick, Frederick County, Maryland, USA

❦ Susanna Anderson (1747–1810)

Born: 1747 Wilmington, New Castle County, Delaware, USA

Died: 1810 Dickson, Dickson County, Tennessee, USA

❦ Mary Anderson (1748–1785)

Born: 2 April 1748 Christina Hundred, New Sweden (Delaware), USA

Died: 1785 Simpson County, Kentucky, USA

❦ Peter Anderson Jr. (1750–1840)

Born: 27 September 1750 New Castle County, New Sweden (Delaware), USA

Died: January 1840 Allen County, Kentucky, USA

🏠 Residences

1707-1738: Lived in the Swedish American enclave of Fort Christina and Wilmington, Delaware—part of the New Sweden colony

❤️ Legacy

Kerstin Christina Elizabeth Derrickson was part of the early Swedish Lutheran community in colonial Delaware. Her marriage to Peter Andersson united two prominent New Sweden families, and through her children—especially Ericus Auricus Anderson—she became a foundational figure in the Anderson family's migration to Tennessee and beyond.

Kerstin Christina Elizabeth Derrickson, born 1707 at Fort Christina, Delaware. A Swedish American matriarch whose legacy lives on through the Anderson family's deep colonial roots. Image or document courtesy of Ancestry.com.

****

Ericus Jöransson Andersson : Old Swede's Churchyard

"The Swedish Emigrant"

Born in 1666 at Fort Christina, New Castle, Delaware—then part of the Swedish colony of New Sweden—Ericus Jöransson Andersson was the first in your line to be born on

American soil. His father, Anders Jöransson, had crossed the Atlantic from Sweden in the mid-1600s, and Ericus inherited both his name and his pioneering spirit.

Ericus came of age in a world still raw with possibility. The Delaware River was his childhood horizon, and the forests of colonial America were both playground and proving ground. He married Brita Paulsson in May 1693, and together they raised a family that would stretch across centuries. Their children included Peter Anderson (b. 1706)—your sixth great-grandfather—and several others who helped root the Anderson name in American soil.

He lived a century—passing away in 1765 at the age of 99—and witnessed the transformation of the colonies from scattered settlements to a society on the brink of revolution. He was buried near Brandywine Creek, near to where he was born, his life a full circle drawn in faith, family, and quiet endurance.

Ericus was not a man of headlines, but of heritage. His legacy was not loud, but lasting. In every Anderson who followed—those who tilled Tennessee clay, who fought in wars, who authored stories and raised children—his blood runs steady. He was the hinge between Old World and New, and the first heartbeat of your American story.

💕 Ericus Joransson Andersson (1671–1765)

Born: May 13, 1671 - Fort Christina, New Castle County, Delaware, United States Died: March 25, 1765 - Brandywine Creek, New Castle County, Delaware Burial: Old Swedes Churchyard, Wilmington, Delaware

🍃 Family

Parents: Anders Joransson (1645-1683) & Sophia Paulsson (1635-1717)

Spouse: Brita Bridget Paulsson (1671-1750), married December 26, 1687, in New Castle, Delaware

Children:

❖Margareta Eriksdotter

Born: 19 November 1689

Died: 20 December 1719

❖Olle Ericksson Joransson Anderson

Born: 1694 • Brandywine Creek, New Castle County, Delaware, USA

Died: 28 August 1778 • New Castle, New Castle County, Delaware

❖Hans Eriksson

Born: 23 March 1696 • Brandywine Creek, New Castle County, Delaware

Died: Unknown

❖Christina Andersson

Born: 1700's • New Castle, Delaware, USA

Died: 1753 • New Castle County, Delaware, USA

❖John Andersson

Born: 1700's • Delaware, United States

Died: 1789 • Wilkes County, North Carolina, United States

❋ Bridget Andersson

Born: 1700's • Christiana Hundred, New Castle County, Delaware, USA

Died: 7 May 1756 • New Castle, New Castle County, Delaware,

❋ William Andersson

Born: 1702 • Fort Christina, New Castle County, Delaware,

Died: 12 December 1776 • Fort Christina, New Castle County, Delaware,

❋ James Anderson

Born: 1703 • Brandywine Creek, New Castle County, Delaware, USA

Died: 12 December 1776 • Wilmington, New Castle County, Delaware,

❋ Peter Ericsson Andersson

Born: 1706 • Fort Christina, New Castle County, Delaware, USA

Died: 26 February 1787 • Orange County, North Carolina, USA

❋ Kerstin Andersson

Born: 3 December 1713 • Wilmington, New Castle County, Delaware, USA

Died: 1793 • New Castle, New Castle County, Delaware, USA

❋ Joseph Andersson

Born: Date unknown • Fort Christina, New Castle County, Delaware, USA Died: 1772 • St. Georges Hundred, New Castle County,

🏠 Residences

1671-1765: Lived in Christina Hundred and Brandywine Creek, Delaware—part of the Swedish American enclave of New Sweden

🏛 Faith & Community

Ericus was baptized, married, and buried at Old Swedes Church, a cornerstone of the Swedish Lutheran community in colonial Delaware. He lived through the transition from Swedish to British rule and helped preserve Swedish cultural identity in the Americas.

Ericus Joransson Andersson, born 1671 at Fort Christina, Delaware. A patriarch of the Anderson family and a pillar of the Swedish American community at Old Swedes Church. Image or document courtesy of Ancestry.co

🎗 Brita Bridget Paulsson (1671–1750)

Born: 1671 - Fort Christina, New Castle County, Delaware, United States Died: March 6, 1750 - Wilmington, New Castle County, Delaware, British Colonies Burial: Old Swedes Churchyard, Wilmington, Delaware

🌿 Family

Parents: Olle Paulsson (1655–1699) & Christina L. Olsen (1652–1726)

Spouse: Ericus Joransson Andersson (1671–1765), married December 26, 1687, in New Castle, Delaware

🏠 Residences

1671-1750: Lived in Christina Hundred and Wilmington, Delaware—part of the Swedish American enclave of New Sweden

⛪ Faith & Community

Brita was baptized, married, and buried at Old Swedes Church, a spiritual and cultural center for the Swedish Lutheran community in colonial Delaware. Her life was one of faith, family, and resilience in a time of shifting colonial powers and frontier challenges.

Parents:

💝 Olle Paulsson

Born: 1655 • Liden, Dalarna, Sweden Died: 4 July 1699 • Feren Hook, New Castle County, Delaware,

💝 Christina L. Olsen

Born: 1652 • Sheephook, New Castle County, Delaware, USA Died: 23 May 1726 • New Castle, New Castle County, Delaware,

From Sweden to the Americas

Olle Paulsson was born in Liden, a parish in Dalarna, a culturally rich and mountainous region of central Sweden.

Likely emigrated as part of the later waves of Swedish settlers to New Sweden, the colonial outpost along the Delaware River.

Settled in Feren Hook (also spelled Forn Höök or Forn Hook), a Swedish community near present-day New Castle, Delaware

Christina L. Olsen was born in Sheephook, a Swedish settlement near Fort Christina, part of the New Sweden colony.

Lived through the transition from Swedish to Dutch and then British rule in the Delaware Valley.

Widowed in 1699 upon the death of her husband, Olle Paulsson, in Feren Hook.

Died in New Castle in 1726, having witnessed the early shaping of colonial society in America.

🌿 Legacy

Brita Bridget Paulsson carried the family's Swedish heritage into the next generation, marrying into the Andersson family and raising a large family in New Castle County, Delaware.

Through Brita, the Paulsson-Olsen lineage became foundational to the Anderson family legacy that would stretch from Delaware to North Carolina and eventually Tennessee.

Landing of the Swedes

In late 1637, the New Sweden Company sent out its first expedition to America to establish a Swedish presence in the New World. Sailing in two ships, the *Kalmar Nyckel* and the *Fogel Grip*, the expedition landed near this site in March 1638. Under Peter Minuit's leadership, Fort Christina was erected to protect the new settlement. Named after Queen Christina of Sweden, the fort was home to approximately 25 colonists. It was the first permanent European settlement in what is now the State of Delaware. Fort Christina served as the new colony's administrative and commercial center as the Swedes expanded their influence throughout the Delaware Valley. Known as New Sweden, the colony was conquered by the Dutch in 1655 before the English took over the region in 1664. Today, the City of Wilmington traces its roots from this first settlement of the Swedes.

DELAWARE PUBLIC ARCHIVES•2013   NCC-197

"The Origin Point"

In the dim light of a Swedish forge, Anders Jöransson raised sons with strong backs and sharper minds. A blacksmith by trade and a farmer by necessity lived in a time when survival was a craft. His prayers were practical, his love worn like a leather apron—quiet, steady, and enduring.

Though little is known of his early life, his name tells us much: Jöransson, meaning "son of Jöran" (the Swedish form of George), places him firmly in the patronymic tradition of 17th-century Sweden. Whether he crossed the Atlantic himself or sent his sons to seek new soil, Anders was the spark that lit the Anderson legacy.

He never saw the Delaware River or the red clay of Tennessee. But the values he forged—resilience, faith, craftsmanship—crossed oceans and centuries. His son, Ericus Jöransson Andersson, would become the first of your line born in the Americas, carrying Anders's name and spirit into a new chapter of history.

And so, while Anders may never have known America, America came to know him—in every beam his descendants raised, every hymn they sang, every story they passed down. He is not just the beginning of a name. He is the beginning of a legacy.

Would you like me to expand this with historical context about 17th-century Dallands or the Swedish migration patterns that may have shaped his family's journey? I can also help you build a visual "root page" for Anders to open your family tree section in Manuscript.

⚓ Anders Joransson (1645–1683)

Born: December 1645 – Gothenburg, Västra Götaland, Sweden Died: May 1683 – Christina Hundred, New Sweden (now Wilmington, Delaware, USA) Burial: At or near Old Swedes Church, Wilmington, Delaware

🧬 Family

Parents: Joran of Sweden (1625–1713) & Sara Larsdotter (1624–1722)

Spouse: Sophia Paulsson (1635–1717), married circa 1648 in Korsholm, Vasa, Finland

Children:

❉ Christiern Andersson Joransson

Born: 1660 • Fort Christina, New Sweden (now Wilmington), Delaware, USA

Died: 23 July 1723 • St. Georges Hundred, New Castle County, Delaware, USA

🌟 James Andersson

Born: 1662 • New Castle, Delaware, USA

Died: 20 April 1717 • Red Lyon Hundred, New Castle County, Delaware, USA

🌟 Peter Joransson Andersson

Born: 1664 • New Sweden, Delaware, USA

Died: 7 April 1750 • Red Lyon Hundred, New Castle County, Delaware, USA

🌟 Joran Andersson

Born: 1666 • Fort Christina, New Castle County, Delaware, USA

Died: 23 July 1718 • New Castle County, Delaware, USA

🌟 Ericus Joransson Andersson

Born: 13 May 1671 • Fort Christina, New Castle County, Delaware, USA

Died: 25 March 1765 • Brandywine Creek, New Castle County, Delaware, USA

🌟 Jons Joransson

Born: 1675 • New Sweden, Delaware, USA

Died: 7 April 1750 • Red Lyon Hundred, New Castle County, Delaware, USA

✂ Migration & Settlement

Arrival: 1671 – Delaware Bay or River, part of the Swedish migration to New Sweden

Settlement: Christina Hundred, New Castle County, Delaware—an area rich in Swedish American heritage

🏠 Legacy

Anders Joransson was part of the second wave of Swedish settlers in the Delaware Valley, arriving just after the fall of New Sweden to the Dutch and later the English. Despite the political shifts, Swedish families like the Joransson maintained their language, customs, and Lutheran faith. Anders helped establish a multigenerational legacy that would stretch from colonial Delaware to the Tennessee frontier.

📷 Suggested Photo Caption

Anders Joransson, born 1645 in Gothenburg, Sweden. A Swedish immigrant to New Sweden whose descendants helped shape the Anderson family's American story. Image or document courtesy of Ancestry.com.

🌷 Sophia Paulsson (1635–1717)

Born: 1635 - Västmanland, Sverige (Sweden) Died: December 9, 1717 - Fort Christina, New Castle County, Delaware, United States Burial: At or near Old Swedes Church, Wilmington, Delaware

🍬 Family

Parents: Olle Paulsson (1600-1650) & Kerstin Paulsonn (1615-1726)

⚓ *Kalmar Nyckel* – The Ship That Carried a Legacy

"She was no grand galleon, but to those aboard, she was a vessel of hope. The Kalmar Nyckel was more than a ship—it was a lifeline between the Old World and the New."

Launched in 1625, the *Kalmar Nyckel* was a Swedish-built pinnace that made four transatlantic voyages between 1638 and 1644—more than any other colonial ship of her time. She brought the first settlers of New Sweden to the Delaware River Valley, anchoring near what would become Fort Christina (modern-day Wilmington, Delaware).

Among those who followed in her wake was **Anders Jöransson**, who arrived in the Delaware Colony as an indentured servant. Though his name may not appear in ship manifests from the earliest voyages, family tradition and oral history hold that he came aboard a later journey of the *Kalmar Nyckel*, or a sister vessel in the Swedish fleet.

"For Anders, the ship was not just a passage, it was a turning point. From the deck of the Kalmar Nyckel, he stepped into a life of labor, liberty, and legacy."

Today, a replica of the *Kalmar Nyckel* sails from Wilmington, Delaware, preserving the memory of those early Swedish settlers whose quiet courage helped shape the American story.

Joran of Sweden (1625-1713)

Born: 1625 – Skinnskatteberg, Västmanland, Sweden Died: October 10, 1713 – Klastorp, Halland, Sweden Burial: In Halland County, Sweden (exact cemetery unconfirmed)

🍖 Family

Parents: Hans Goransson (1608-1672) & Ingrid Nilsdotter (1610-1689)

Spouse: Sara Larsdotter (1624-1722)

Children:

Anders Joransson (1645-1683) – your eighth great-grandfather, who emigrated to New Sweden (Delaware)

🏠 Residences

1625-1670s: Skinnskatteberg, Västmanland, Sweden – a region known for its ironworks, historic mining town in Västmanland, known for its ironworks and deep forested landscapes.

Later Years: Klastorp, Halland County, Sweden – where he passed away at the age of eighty-eight.

🌐 Legacy

Joran lived through the height of Sweden's Age of Greatness, a time when the Swedish Empire was a major European power. Though he remained in Sweden, his son Anders Joransson would emigrate to the Americas, becoming one of the early settlers of New

Sweden in Delaware. Through that lineage, Joran became the patriarch of the Anderson family in America.

🪶 Sara Larsdotter (1624–1722)

Born: February 8, 1624 – Övre Darsbo, Skinnskatteberg, Västmanland, Sweden Died: March 26, 1722 – Nedre Sunnanfors, Skinnskatteberg, Västmanland, Sweden Burial: In Skinnskatteberg Parish, Västmanland, Sweden

🦌 Deer Point: The Legacy of Anders Jöransson

West of Christina, New Sweden — 1672-1678

In the autumn of 1672, a Swedish settler named Anders Jöransson made a defining investment in the Americas. On September 27, he purchased part of a plantation known as Deer Point, a tract of land nestled west of Christina (present-day Wilmington, Delaware). The seller was Sinnick Broer, a Swedish Finn whose name would later become entwined with the Jöransson family in many ways.

Deer Point was more than a parcel of land—it was a foothold in a fragile colonial world. The Swedish presence in the Delaware Valley had already weathered conquest by the Dutch and, later, the English. Yet families like the Jöranssons persisted, carving out lives along the riverbanks, raising children, and planting roots in the soil of a contested frontier.

In June 1675, Anders and an English partner purchased 540 acres south of the Cohansey River in what is now New Jersey. It was a bold move, signaling ambition and expansion. But fate intervened. Anders Jöransson died before the relocation could take place. His widow, Sophia, sold his interest in the New Jersey property in February 1675/1676, just months after his passing.

Sophia's story did not end in widowhood. She remarried—this time to Broer Sinnicksson, the very man who had sold Anders the Deer Point land. On May 8, 1678, Broer was formally granted Anders' former property at Deer Point. But this transfer came with a solemn obligation: Broer promised to pay five hundred Dutch guilders to each of Anders,' that were living, when they reached the age of twenty-one.

The payments Broer made over the years not only fulfilled a legal obligation—they preserved a father's legacy. They ensured that Anders' children would inherit not just land or money, but a place in the story of New Sweden. His eldest son, Christiern, was naturalized by William Penn in 1683. His fourth son, Eric, would go on to purchase land of his own and raise a family whose descendants would carry the Anderson name deep into the American frontier.

Deer Point may no longer appear on modern maps, but its legacy endures—in the land, in the records, and in the lives of those who trace their roots to that quiet bend west of Christina.

❧ Final Chapter: The Inheritance of Memory

The concluding chapter is not a period—it is a passing of the pen.

As I close this book, I do not close the story. I simply place a marker in the long, unfolding narrative of the Anderson family. The names etched into these pages—Ericus, Peter, Nathaniel, Helen, Robert—are not just ancestors. They are echoes. They are the soil from which I grew.

I have walked the fields they once plowed. I stood beneath the same Tennessee sky. I have heard their voices in the rush of morning and the creak of old floorboards. And now, I offer their stories to you—not as relics, but as roots.

This book is not the end. It is a beginning for those who come next. May you read these pages and feel not just history, but home. May you carry forward the grit, the grace, and the quiet strength that defines what it means to be an Anderson.

And when your time comes to add your own chapter, may you do so with reverence, with courage, and with love.

"We are not the end of the story. We are the ones holding the pen."

The Anderson family story does not conclude with this book—it continues in the breath of every descendant, in the soil of every Tennessee ridge, and in the quiet strength passed from hand to hand like a family heirloom.

This manuscript began as a search for names and dates. But what emerged was something far more sacred: a rediscovery of identity. These pages are not just filled with ancestors—they are filled with echoes. With voices that once sang lullabies, whispered prayers, and told stories by firelight. With footsteps that crossed oceans, tilled red clay, and marched into war. With hearts that endured hardship, celebrated harvests, and loved with a depth that defied time.

I have walked the paths they once walked. I have stood in the cemeteries where their names are etched in stone. I held their photographs, their letters, their stories—and in doing so, I held them.

But this book is not mine alone. It belongs to every child who wonders where they came from. To every grandchild who hears a name and asks, "Who was that?" It belongs to the future—to those not yet born who will one day trace their roots back to these pages and find not just history, but home.

So, I leave this not as a conclusion, but as a charge:
So, if you are holding this book now, know this: you are not just a reader, you are a continuation. A living branch on a tree rooted in grit, grace, and memory. May you carry these stories forward, not as burdens, but as blessings. And when your time happens them on, may you do so with the same reverence that brought them here.

Because the story of the Andersons is not finished. It lives on—in you.

This is where the ink runs quietly. Where names once whispered now rest in full voice, and the dust of memory settles like morning light on the shoulders of those who dared to remember. If the front of this book was a door opening, let this be the porch light left on— a signal to the next soul who comes searching. Because legacy is not a thing we own. It is a thing we tend to do. So, take these stories, these names, these truths— and carry them forward. Not as burden. But as a blessing. We endure. We rise. We remember. —Brian Keith Anderson the Keeper of Memory

Comprehensive Index

Abb Anderson 30, 31

Adams Family 34, 35, 56, 58

Adams, Aubrey Lee 58

Adams, Helen Maxine 34, 35

Adams, Robert Taylor 56

Anderson Family 8, 19, 23, 30, 32, 41, 60

Anderson, Anders Jöransson 14, 15

Anderson, Brian Keith 60, 61

Anderson, Edgar 27, 28

Anderson, Ericus 16, 17

Anderson, John Watson 23, 24

Anderson, Nathaniel Hamilton 25, 26

Anderson, Robert Kenneth Sr. 32, 33

Bennett Family 64

Brown Family 70, 71

Brown, Bessie Mae 72

Coffee County, Tennessee 19, 23, 41, 45

Fort Christina (Delaware) 12, 16

Henry's Cove 19, 41, 42

Hillsboro, Tennessee 23, 27, 30, 34, 41

Jones, Harriet E. 27

Manchester, Tennessee 42, 72

McMinnville, Tennessee 60

Meadows Family 64

Phillips Family 30, 31, 75

Phillips, George Washington 76

Phillips, Robert Calvin 75

Phillips, Willie Jane 30, 31

Poff Family 77, 78

Poff, Gracie Ann 75, 78

Poff, James Marshall 78

Sweden 12, 14

Tennessee 8, 19, 23, 41, 45, 60, 72

Woodall Grain Company 43

Zumbro Family 64

www.ingramcontent.com/pod-product-compliance
Lightning Source LLC
Chambersburg PA
CBHW020544030426
42337CB00013B/971